D1595439

CHRISTIANS FOR FREEDOM

IN CANTIC
IN EPISTOLAS PAULI
GREGOR. X.
BVCERVS.
L. Gaultier incidit.
EFFIGIES D. THOMÆ AQVINATIS:
Quem Ecclesia Doctorem, scholæ magistrum, hæreticj flagellum habuere: quemq;
Pius Papa V. quintum Ecclesiæ Doctorem nominare solebat. Hunc Italia
nascentem vidit, sanguinis nobilitas celebrauit. Auus eius fuit Comes
Sommacolensis, quj Fredericj II. Imp. sorore ducta Landulphum progenuit,
cuj Theodora Comitis Theanensis filia Sanctum Thomam peperit.

CHRISTIANS FOR FREEDOM
LATE-SCHOLASTIC ECONOMICS

by
ALEJANDRO ANTONIO CHAFUEN

With a Foreword by
MICHAEL NOVAK

IGNATIUS PRESS   SAN FRANCISCO

Cover photo of the University of Salamanca
and cover design by Roxanne Mei Lum

© 1986 Ignatius Press, San Francisco
ISBN 0-89870-110-4
Library of Congress catalogue number 86-80784
Printed in the United States of America

Totus Tuus—Ad Sancta Maria, Mater Dei

CONTENTS

FOREWORD

The role of Catholic thinkers in Spain in anticipating many of the insights of classical economics, although known to a few economic historians, is not well known to the intellectual community as a whole. The breadth and depth of those anticipations, made evident here in the extensive quotations brought to focus by Alejandro Antonio Chafuen, are of extraordinary importance, since the influence of Spain upon Latin America remains crucial even today.

Some of the roots of classical liberal thought, Dr. Chafuen shows, lie in Spain, in the great Spanish Late Scholastics, particularly of the Salamanca school. Through Protestant writers like Samuel Pufendorf (1632–1694), some of the arguments of the Salamanca school appeared in the course of study Francis Hutcheson established for Adam Smith, and the latter from time to time alluded to them in his works. In fact, the perceptions and formulations of the Salamanca school helped to establish the broad tradition and the "common sense" to which British liberals loved to appeal, portraying themselves, not as revolutionary thinkers, but as systematizers of the common experience of the ages.

Chafuen helps us to see that by the end of the seventeenth century, the common teachings of the Spanish Late Scholastics had already established many of the rudimentary presuppositions we now take to be "liberal" or "capitalist". That this is true concerning private property will not come as much of a surprise (although the Late Scholastic critique of a system of goods held in common is surprisingly sharp). However, the "liberal" views of the Late Scholastics on public finance, the theory of money, the theory of value, price theory, wages and profits are quite arresting. While matters of economics were not the chief focus of their work, it is startling to see how "modern" their formulations seem. That they were men of experience, with a sharp eye for "the way the world works", is made abundantly clear in the scores of quotations Chafuen has collected.

Moreover, the Late Scholastics attached crucial importance to commerce as a work of community and peace. Commercial activity was, for them, a daily expression of the common good. They praised the contributions of tradesmen and merchants for fulfilling an important part of the divine purpose, through the daily service of human betterment. God made the regions of the world diverse, one of them opined, so that the common good would be served through exchange.

Given Church teachings on the infertility of money and, therefore, on the immorality of interest (usury), it remains true that the Late Scholastics felt bound to treat the taking of interest more warily than did later capitalist thinkers. Still, they discerned many legitimate forms of interest. They even glimpsed its basic principle, seeing clearly enough that borrowed funds, matched with hard work and inventiveness, could and did produce new wealth; hence, money is not entirely infertile. Although they never succeeded in overturning the ancient doctrine of the sterility of money, they began, case by case, laying the groundwork that others were later to build upon.

Dr. Chafuen is modest and careful in stating conclusions; perhaps, given the range of his research, he is too cautious. He contents himself with the role of saying, in effect: "Here are large collections of textual materials that deserve careful and painstaking study. They have been too much neglected. They deserve fuller and more detailed investigation." And yet even the preliminary evidence Dr. Chafuen has assembled suggests that we will have to revise some of our assumptions about the role of Catholic scholarship in the history of the free economy. Clearly, the Late Scholastics walked at least in the direction of the revolution in economic thought that later reached its fruition in the eighteenth century.

In passing, Dr. Chafuen demolishes the odd (but well-known) opinion of R. H. Tawney that Thomas Aquinas, like Marx, held to the "labor theory of value". Chafuen supplies numerous texts showing how Aquinas and his followers, at least in Spain, taught that such a theory injures the common good. It is not sufficient, or even fair, for value to be established solely in the light of labor and other costs. In their eyes, economic value depends upon many other factors, as they easily made plain from experience and common sense.

This little study abounds with brilliant aphorisms and short quotations, many of which are as exactly apposite for economic activities today as they were four centuries ago. What the reader will especially appreciate is their ring of common sense. Permit me to highlight a few of them, from an abundance of riches:

ON COMMON OWNERSHIP

Evil men will take more and add less to the barn of the common goods.
                                        —*Francisco de Vitoria*

Each worker will try to appropriate as many goods as possible, and given the way human beings desire riches, everyone will behave in the same fashion. The peace, tranquility and friendship sought by the philosophers will thus inevitably be subverted.
                                        —*Domingo de Soto, 1567*

We cannot find a person who does not favor his own interests, or who does not prefer to furnish his home rather than that of the republic. We can see that privately owned property flourishes, while city- and council-owned property suffers from inadequate care and worse management. In this regard, Aristotle states that the pleasure a man feels while working at his own business is inevitable. It is not easy to explain how important it is for man to know that he is the owner of the thing he produces. On the other hand, people treat common enterprises with great indifference. . . . After man's loss of innocence, it becomes necessary for each individual to share in the things of this world, in real estate or moveable riches. . . . If universal love won't induce people to take care of things, private interest will. Hence, privately owned goods will multiply. Had they remained in common possession, the opposite would be true.   —*Tomas de Mercado, 1571*

A donkey owned by many wolves is soon eaten.
                                —*proverb often cited by the Late Scholastics*

We know that the fields are not going to be efficiently tilled in common ownership, and that there will not be peace in the republic, so we see that it is efficient to undertake the division of goods.
                                        —*Domingo de Bañez, 1594*

... private property is necessary for human life for three reasons: "First, because each person takes more trouble to care for something that is his sole responsibility than what is held in common or by many—for in such a case each individual shirks the work and leaves the responsibility to somebody else, which is what happens when too many officials are involved. Second, because human affairs are more efficiently organized if each person has his own responsibility to discharge; there would be chaos if everybody cared for everything. Third, because men live together in greater peace where everyone is content with his own (*re sua contentus est*). We do, in fact, notice that quarrels often break out amongst men who hold things in common without distinction."

—St. Thomas Aquinas, Summa, II–II, qu. 66, art. 2, resp.

ON PUBLIC FINANCE

The origin of poverty is high taxes. In continual fear of tax collectors, [farmers] prefer to abandon their land, so they can avoid their vexations. As King Teodorico said, the only agreeable country is one where no man is afraid of tax collectors.

—Pedro Fernandez Navarrete, 1619

He who imposes high taxes receives from very few.   *—Ibid.*

The king is not going to be poor if the vassals are rich, because riches are better kept in the hands of the subjects than in the thrice-locked coffins of the State Treasurers, who go bankrupt daily.

—Ibid.

ON PROFIT

Those who measure the just price by the labor, costs and risk incurred by the person who deals in the merchandise or produces it, or by the cost of transport, or the expense of travelling to and from the fair, or by what he has to pay the factors for their industry, risk and labor, are greatly in error, and still more so are those who allow a certain profit of a fifth or tenth. For the just price arises from the abundance or scarcity of goods, merchants and money, as has been said, and not from costs, labor and risk. If we had to consider labor and risk in order to assess the just price, no merchants would ever

suffer a loss, nor would abundance or scarcity of goods and money
enter into the question.   —*Luis Savaria de la Calle*

Among the motives which justify profits, St. Thomas mentioned
the following: (1) To provide for the businessman's household;
(2) To help the poor; (3) To ensure that the country does not run
short of essential supplies; (4) To compensate the businessman's
work; (5) To improve the merchandise. . . . He also ascribed legitimacy to profits obtained from price variations in response to local
changes as well as those earned through the lapse of time. Furthermore, he allowed for profits which would compensate the risks
of transport and delivery.   —*Summary of II–II, qu. 77, art. 4, reply.*

Anglo-American readers tend to forget that, at the height of its
power, Spain was awash with new commercial activities and extended
international trading. Until France and Great Britain caught up, few
national populations had as much experience with economic activities
of comparable scope, novelty and complexity. Moralists close to the
lay persons involved had entire new bodies of human experience to
contend with, both in the Old World and in the New. Well taught by
Aristotle and Aquinas in the ways of common sense, in a morality
based upon practical wisdom and alert to circumstances, contingen-
cies and consequences, the Late Scholastics were well placed to think
broadly and concretely. The examples and the cases they used showed
a lively interest in realistic detail.

Of few books can it be said that they open our eyes to new bodies
of material and to an important revision of long-held views. This
short study by Dr. Chafuen is such a book. If further studies vindicate
the promise he has opened up, the Catholic Church will gain by a
deeper understanding of her own tradition, and she will achieve a
clearer sense of her own slow but steady journey toward liberty, in
the economic as well as in the political domain.

Finally, Dr. Chafuen's knowledge of the tradition of the Austrian
school of classical economics allows him, in his last lengthy chapter, to
examine the economic thought of the Late Scholastics in its light. The
Anglo-American economic tradition is not neglected in Latin America,
but the Austrian school appears to be of even greater importance to its

theoreticians. In the years ahead, this linking of the Austrian school to the commonsense observations of the Late Scholastics of Salamanca may be a significant event in Latin American intellectual life.

Michael Novak
August 26, 1985

PREFACE

I owe a great part of my education to a college supported by an outstanding man and an outstanding Christian, the late J. Howard Pew. In his will, dated November 11, 1963, he expressed a wish which I share. Mr. Pew wanted his estate to support institutions with the following educational objectives:

> To acquaint the American people with the evils of bureaucracy and the vital need to maintain and preserve a limited form of government in the United States as intended by our forebears and expressed by them in the Constitution and the Bill of Rights—to point out the dangerous consequences that result from an exchange of our American priceless heritage of freedom and self-determination for the false promises of Socialism and a planned economy—to expose the insidious influences which have infiltrated many of our channels of publicity—and to inform our people of the struggle, persecution, hardship, sacrifice and death by which freedom of the individual was won.
>
> To acquaint the American people with the values of a free-market—the dangers of inflation—the need for a stable monetary standard—the paralyzing effects of government controls on the lives and activities of the people—and the necessity of maintaining the rights as provided in the Bill of Rights.
>
> *To promote recognition of the interdependence of Christianity and freedom and to support and expound the philosophy that we must first have faith in God before we can enjoy the blessings of liberty—for God is the author of liberty—and to bring about the realization that our failure to fight for the preservation of our liberty is a crime, the punishment for which is servitude.*[1]

The major objective of this thesis is to study the contributions of

---

[1] Mary Sennholz, *Faith and Freedom: A Biographical Sketch of a Great American, John Howard Pew* (Grove City, Penn.: Grove City College, 1975), pp. 170–171.

Roman Catholic writers to the understanding and furtherance of the free society, especially in the field of economics. It also embraces the objective of J. Howard Pew: "To promote recognition of the interdependence of Christianity and freedom" . . . not only for American people, but for all peoples.

It is not unusual to find Catholic authors who oppose economic freedom. Some believe that the free market contradicts Christian teachings. Others subscribe to the notion that a free economic system cannot achieve "desirable" ends. Still others reject it on the authority of their priests, pastors or moralists whom they happen to meet in daily life.

This study is directed to all those people, Catholic or non-Catholic, who believe that the free market is incompatible with Christianity. It is intended, as well, for all those who believe that economic freedom is an essential aspect of human liberty.

Many intellectuals have pulled away from Christianity in the belief that God's representatives on earth preach against reason and freedom. The new attitudes of the Church toward scientific freedom may help to modify this situation. It is my hope that this study will shed more light on the topic of late Medieval economic thought, assist moralists toward greater understanding of how the free-market system works and remind free-market proponents of the Christian values that undergird "their" system.

The most recent decades of the twentieth century have brought important advances in the history of economic thought. The Roman Catholic writers of the late Middle-Ages—the so-called Late Scholastic authors—have been the focus of considerable study and re-evaluation. Their works offer insight into the issue of personal freedom. This study attempts an analysis of the theoretical context in which the Scholastics wrote, especially when they addressed the issues of private property, sound money and government intervention. Many of their works are applicable to discussion of "the free society" and may contribute to a more thorough understanding of the development of modern economic thought. Scholastic writings also shed light on many concepts that apply to the foundation of a social order respectful of personal freedom.

ACKNOWLEDGMENTS

The support of many people made this study possible. To begin with, I want to remember my parents, who gave all they had to provide their children with the best possible education, and to express my sincere gratitude to them.

Several institutions provided the material support for each of the necessary stages of my research. In 1978, the *Centro de Estudios sobre la Libertad* (Buenos Aires, Argentina) awarded me a scholarship to study under Dr. Hans F. Sennholz at Grove City College (Pennsylvania). The *Fundacion Perez Companc* (Buenos Aires) underwrote my transportation to Toledo, Spain, in 1982 and to Grove City in 1984. My studies in Spain were supported by a joint grant (in August 1982) from the *Fundacion Ortega y Gasset* (Spain) and the *Instituto Torcuato Di Tella* (Argentina). In 1984, I received a scholarship from Grove City College, which allowed me to complete my project. Throughout the course of my studies, the E.S.E.A.D.E. (*Escuela Superior de Economia y Administracion de Empresas,* Buenos Aires) gave me great assistance. Its dean and founder, Dr. Alberto Benegas Lynch, Jr., encouraged me to pursue my endeavors. The staff at E.S.E.A.D.E.'s Research Department (Dr. Ezequiel Gallo, Dr. Juan Carlos Cachanosky, Lic. Alfredo Irigoin, Gabriel Zanotti and Lic. Eduardo Zimmerman) assisted me with important comments on the subject matter of my research.

Many individuals contributed to my work. Dr. Oreste Popescu of the faculty at the Universidad Catolica Argentina awakened my interest in the subject. Dr. Manuel Rio (of the *Academia Nacional de Ciencias Morales y Politicas* [Buenos Aires], and of the *Academie Nationale Française*) and Lic. Jose Mario Juan Cravero (Universidad Catolica Argentina) pointed out its importance. Franciscan Father Antolin Abad (of Toledo, Spain) generously assisted my research by allowing me free access to the bibliographical treasures of the scholastic library at San

Juan de los Reyes Monastery. Above all, I am grateful for the constant help and support of my teacher and tutor, Dr. Hans F. Sennholz.

During the editing process, Dr. De Velde and the computer department staff of Grove City College helped me with a true Christian spirit. The atmosphere created in this spirit is the greatest support an intellectual can have. It characterizes all the people who work at the college—from the staff of the Henry Buhl Library to the members of the College administration. Miss Cindy Forrester was not only my English supervisor, but also my advisor as to the structure and consistency of my work. She improved each page of the study. Miss Melanie Bailey gave me her generous help in the final correction of the manuscript.

I must also mention the aid I received from my spiritual friends. God's presence and the sweet arms of His Son supported me in the moments of hardship. The Truth is His; the mistakes are mine.

PART ONE

THE LATE SCHOLASTICS

1

THE LATE SCHOLASTICS

Medieval Scholasticism encompassed some seven centuries, from 800 A.D. to 1500 A.D. The twelfth and thirteen centuries constitute the most widely recognized period of Scholastic activity. The activity of the period from 1350 to 1500 A.D. is known as Late Scholasticism. Although many authors speak of a decline in Scholastic thought after the fourteenth century, its importance did not wane until the late seventeenth century.

The term *Scholastic* refers to teachers and authors who employed the Scholastic method. It is derived from the Latin word *schola* (school), which

> was essentially a rational investigation of every relevant problem in liberal arts, philosophy, theology, medicine, and law, examined from opposing points of view, in order to reach an intelligent, scientific solution that would be consistent with accepted authorities, known facts, human reason, and Christian faith.[1]

The ultimate goal of Scholasticism was to formulate a corpus of scientific thought applicable to all areas of life. The Medieval School-men or, as they preferred to be called, the "Doctors", were the foremost thinkers of their times. Their analyses and conclusions shaped Catholic thinking so persuasively that they continue to be a significant foundation of contemporary Church doctrine.

---

[1] *New Catholic Encyclopedia* (New York: McGraw-Hill, 1967), s.v. "Scholastic Method", by J. A. Weisheipl.

Origins and Influence

I. C. Brady ascribes the origin of Scholasticism to "the use of Aristotelian dialectics in theology, philosophy, and Canon Law".[2] Having been recovered for the Western World through Latin translations from the Arabic versions, Aristotle's ideas were well known to the great majority of Scholastic authors, who also relied on the Old and New Testaments, the works of the "Fathers of the Church" (i.e., Patristic literature) and the writings of the Roman jurists.[3]

St. Thomas Aquinas (1226–1274) was the foremost Scholastic writer. His influence was so widespread that nearly all subsequent Schoolmen studied, quoted and commented upon his remarks. The century following St. Thomas produced many Scholastic authors whose works relate to economics. St. Bernardino of Siena (1380–1444), St. Antonino of Florence (1389–1459), Joannis Gerson (1362–1428), Conradus Summenhart (1465–1511) and Sylvestre de Priero (d. 1523) are perhaps the best known, since they are most frequently quoted by their successors. The writings of Cajetan (Cardinal Tomas de Vio, 1468–1534) represent the transition between these Scholastics and their later Hispanic followers.

The Hispanic Scholastics

Some historians have baptized the Hispanic Scholastics "the authors of the school of Salamanca". Marjorie Grice-Hutchinson devotes an entire chapter of her book *Early Economic Thought in Spain, 1177–1740,* to "The School of Salamanca". Raymond De Roover also speaks of

---

[2] *New Catholic Encyclopedia,* s.v. "Scholasticism", by I. C. Brady.

[3] As, for example, the Roman jurist Paulo. See Bernard W. Dempsey, "Just Price in a Functional Economy", *American Economic Review* 25 (September 1935): 473–474.

"the famous school of Salamanca".[4] While it is true that many of the Hispanic Scholastics studied or taught at Salamanca, it is also true that some of the most important Scholastic authors studied at other Spanish universities, such as the Complutense at Alcalá de Henares. It is therefore more accurate to describe them as "Hispanic Scholastics".[5]

Francisco de Vitoria (c. 1480–1546) is called the Father of the Hispanic Scholastics. He belonged to the Dominican order and studied and taught at the Sorbonne, where he helped to edit one of the editions of Aquinas' *Summa Theologica* and of the *Summa* of Saint Antonino of Florence. From 1522 to 1546, he taught at the University of Salamanca.

Domingo de Soto (1495–1560), also a Dominican, studied at Alcalá and under Vitoria in Paris. After his return to Spain, he taught at Alcalá and in 1532 was appointed professor of theology at Salamanca. His treatise *De Iustitia et Iure* went through no fewer than twenty-seven editions in fifty years and continues to exert significant influence.[6] A new bilingual edition was published in Madrid as recently as 1968.

Another of the early Hispanic Scholastics was Martín de Azpilcueta, "Dr. Navarrus" (1493–1586). Regarded as one of the most eminent canon lawyers of his day, he taught at Salamanca and Coimbra (in Portugal). His *Manual de Confesores y Penitentes*[7] was one of the most widely used spiritual handbooks in the century following its publication. Azpilcueta was also of the Dominican order. Other important Dominican Scholastics include Domingo de Bañez (1528–1604),

---

[4] Marjorie Grice-Hutchinson, *Early Economic Thought in Spain, 1177–1740* (London: Allen & Unwin, 1975); *International Encyclopedia of the Social Sciences* (New York: Free Press, 1968), s.v. "Economic Thought, Ancient and Medieval Thought", by Raymond De Roover.

[5] In his excellent essay, "Aspectos Analíticos en la Doctrina del Justo Precio de Juan de Matienzo (1520–1579)" in *La Economía Como Disciplina Científica: Ensayos en Honor del Profesor Dr. Francisco Valsechi* (Buenos Aires: Macchi, 1982), pp. 235–286, Oreste Popescu challenges the use of this name. My preference for the term "Hispanic Scholastics" is due to Dr. Popescu's convincing arguments.

[6] Grice-Hutchinson, *Early Economic Thought in Spain*, p. 95; Domingo de Soto, *De Iustitia et Iure* (Madrid: IEP, 1968).

[7] Martín de Azpilcueta, *Manual de Confesores y Penitentes* (Salamanca, 1556).

Tomás de Mercado (c. 1500–1575), Francisco García[8] and Pedro de Ledesma.[9]

Scholasticism may not be ascribed to one religious order alone. The Franciscan thinkers Juan de Medina (1490–1546), Luis de Alcalá[10] and Henrique de Villalobos (d. 1637) employed Scholastic sources and methods. The Augustinian bishop Miguel Salón (1538–1620) as well as Pedro de Aragón,[11] Cristobal de Villalón,[12] Luis Saravia de la Calle[13] and Felipe de la Cruz[14] added to the body of Scholastic thought. With the foundation of the Society of Jesus in 1540, Jesuit thinkers such as Luis de Molina (1535–1600), Juan de Mariana (1535–1624), Francisco Suarez (1548–1617), Juan de Salas (1553–1612), Leonardo Lessio (1554–1623), Juan de Lugo (1583–1660), Pedro de Oñate (1567–1646), Juan de Matienzo (1520–1579) and Antonio de Escobar y Mendoza (1589–1669) made significant contributions. Some historians believe that the attitude toward economics espoused by the Late Scholastics was, in fact, the attitude of the Jesuits. H. M. Robertson said, for example, that the Jesuits

> favoured enterprise, freedom of speculation and the expansion of trade as a social benefit. It would not be difficult to claim that the

---

[8] Francisco García, *Tratado Utilísimo de Todos los Contratos, Quantos en los Negocios Humanos se Pueden Ofrecer* (Valencia, 1583).

[9] Pedro de Ledesma, *Summa* (Salamanca, 1614).

[10] Luis de Alcalá, *Tractado de los préstamos que passan entre mercaderes y tractantes, y por consiguiente de los logros, cambios, compras adelantadas, y ventas al fiado* (Toledo: Juan de Ayala, 1543).

[11] Pedro de Aragón, *De Iustitia et Iure* (Lyon, 1596).

[12] Cristobal de Villalón, *Provechoso Tratado de Cambios y Contrataciones de Mercaderes y Reprobacion de Usura* (Valladolid: Francisco Fernandez de Cordoba, 1542).

[13] Luis Saravia de la Calle Veronense, *Instrucción de Mercaderes muy Provechosa* (Medina del Campo, 1544). A modern edition of this work was published in Madrid in 1949.

[14] Felipe de La Cruz, *Tratado Unico de Intereses Sobre si se Puede Llevar Dinero por Prestallo* (Madrid: Francisco Martinez, 1637).

religion which favoured the spirit of capitalism was Jesuitry, not Calvinism.[15]

While Jesuit thought may indeed have encouraged the rise of a system based on private property (post-Marxian authors speak of the capitalist system), it does not follow that the Jesuit authors deserve all the credit (or all the blame, if we look at history through a glass of a different color). Jesuit conclusions, as we shall see, have a long tradition and are rooted in the writings of Aristotle, St. Thomas Aquinas, and their Scholastic followers. The Late Scholastic Jesuits were outstanding, but they were not alone in the intellectual battlefield. They were in the company of the best theologians, jurists and philosophers of their times.

Figure 1 delineates the family tree of the Late Scholastics. It also illustrates the spread of Scholasticism throughout the Western world. Molina and Rebelo exercised considerable influence in Portugal, as did Escobar in France (where the Physiocrats shared many ideas with the Hispanic Scholastics) and Leonardo Lessio (who had a strong influence on Hugo Grotius [1583–1645]) in the Netherlands. Diana (1585–1663) and Bonacina (1585–1663) helped spread Scholasticism in Italy, while Matienzo and Oñate were among those who introduced it in Hispanic America. In Germany the Hispanic Scholastics had a great impact on the writings of Samuel von Pufendorf (1632–1694). Through Grotius, Pufendorf and the Physiocrats, many Late Scholastic ideas influenced Anglo-Saxon economic thought, especially the "Scottish School" consisting of Ferguson (1723–1816), Hutcheson (1694–1746) and Smith (c. 1723–1790).[16]

---

[15] H. M. Robertson, *Aspects of the Rise of Economic Individualism: A Criticism of Max Weber and His School.* New ed. (Clifton: A. M. Kelly, 1973), p. 164.

[16] Adam Smith included many quotations from Grotius and Pufendorf in his *Lectures on Justice.* The works of these two Protestant authors were required textbooks in the courses Adam Smith took with Francis Hutcheson. Adam Smith, *Lectures on Justice, Police, Revenue and Arms, Delivered in the University of Glasgow by Adam Smith, Reported by a Student in 1763* (New York: Kelley & Millman, 1956), p. 177.

Figure 1.

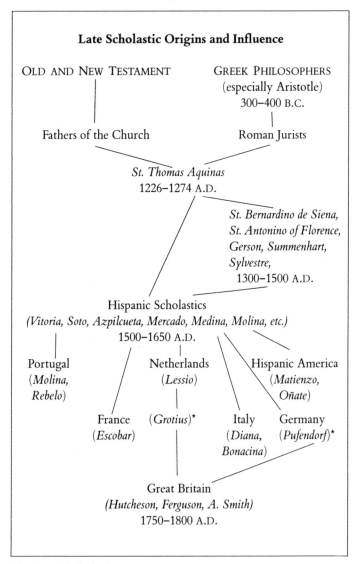

Late Scholastic Origins and Influence

OLD AND NEW TESTAMENT

GREEK PHILOSOPHERS
(especially Aristotle)
300–400 B.C.

Fathers of the Church

Roman Jurists

St. Thomas Aquinas
1226–1274 A.D.

St. Bernardino de Siena,
St. Antonino of Florence,
Gerson, Summenhart,
Sylvestre,
1300–1500 A.D.

Hispanic Scholastics
(Vitoria, Soto, Azpilcueta, Mercado, Medina, Molina, etc.)
1500–1650 A.D.

Portugal
(Molina,
Rebelo)

Netherlands
(Lessio)

Hispanic America
(Matienzo,
Oñate)

France
(Escobar)

(Grotius)★

Italy
(Diana,
Bonacina)

Germany
(Pufendorf)★

Great Britain
(Hutcheson, Ferguson, A. Smith)
1750–1800 A.D.

★Grotius and Pufendorf were Protestants.

2

THE SCHOLASTIC APPROACH TO ECONOMICS

The Middle Ages saw a great proliferation of natural-law doctrines in the post-Aquinas period. For J. Gerson, Conradus Summenhart, St. Bernardino of Siena and St. Antonino of Florence, the concept of natural law was fundamental. Starting with Francisco de Vitoria, the Hispanic Scholastics continued this tradition.[1]

St. Thomas Aquinas defined natural law as the sharing of intellectual creatures in eternal law (*Participatio legis aeternae in rationali creatura*). Eternal law represents God's plan to lead all creation to their final end. From this point of view, a natural moral law constitutes participation by the human intellect in God's plan for what is right, that is, in eternal law.[2] For Thomistic ethics,

> The intelligent use of human understanding is a proximate source of moral law. The intelligent use of human understanding to work out moral laws is called right reasoning. Since right reason is founded on man's nature and the natures of other things in his environment, and since rational appraisal of the suitability or unsuitability of a given action occurs in the natural course of human life, judgments of right reason also are called natural laws.[3]

Aquinas' works were the starting point for most of the Schoolmen. Other authors granted greater importance to the various aspects of natural law. Some treated natural law as something apprehended by

---

[1] Modern authors have ascribed great importance to the writings of Hugo Grotius and Samuel von Pufendorf without analyzing their immediate predecessors, i.e., the Hispanic Scholastics. For example see Henry B. Veatch, "Natural Law: Dead or Alive", *Literature of Liberty* 1 (October–December 1978): pp. 7–31.

[2] St. Thomas Aquinas, *Summa Theologica,* Latin text and English translation (London: Blackfriars, 1975), I–II, qu. 91, art. 2, resp.

[3] *New Catholic Encyclopedia* (New York: McGraw-Hill, 1967), s.v. "Ethics", by V. J. Bourke.

human reason with no need for discursive reasoning. Bañez and most of the Dominican theologians (especially Vitoria and de Soto) considered the principles of natural law to be self-evident (*per se nota*). According to Bañez, natural law consists of self-evident principles and the conclusions that necessarily follow from them. His example was the Golden Rule and its application to private property. From the principle of natural law, "Do unto others as you would have them do unto you", he arrived at the conclusion, "you must not steal".[4]

It is possible to distinguish two branches of natural law in Scholastic reasoning: analytical natural law (also called the laws of nature) and normative natural law. The first type is universal and lies beyond human control. At times, human beings may harness the knowledge of analytical natural law for technical purposes. Even when they do not, they cannot escape its effects. Since analytical natural laws cannot be broken, they do not need to be enforced. In the words of Karl Popper,

> a natural law describes a strict, unvarying regularity which either in fact holds in nature (in this case, the law is a true statement) or does not hold (in this case it is false).[5]

Normative natural laws, on the other hand, lay down precepts for our behavior. They are rules for human conduct. It is possible for human action to violate normative natural laws, but not without serious consequences. Both analytical and normative natural laws are important for economic and social order. The more humans accommodate their actions to both branches of natural law, the greater their prospects for success.

The Late Scholastics assigned great importance to the jurisprudential and ethical aspects of normative natural law. They would have discarded the concept of private property, for instance, if they had not found

---

[4] Domingo de Bañez, *De Iustitia et Iure Decisiones* (Salamanca, 1594), ques. 57, f. 12; see also pp. 39–40.

[5] Karl Popper, *The Open Society and Its Enemies* (Princeton: Princeton University Press, 1950), p. 58. Popper believes in the existence of natural laws of social life, for instance the ones "formulated by modern economic theories". Ibid., p. 68.

this institution to be in agreement with natural law. Although not explicitly defined, the idea of analytical natural law was implicit in all their writings, and it contributed to their concept of the natural order. Their use of empirical and deductive reasoning to demonstrate that scarcity affects prices springs from their assumption of a natural order to which humans must accommodate their actions.

The ethical and juridical (i.e., normative) ideas of natural law are closely related to the analytical concept. The latter is part of the "order of reason". By viewing the relationship between reasonableness and human nature as the Late Scholastics did, we can understand the idea that when a scientific law is true, then it must also be an analytical natural law. St. Thomas Aquinas wrote, "And so whatever is contrary to the order of reason is contrary to the nature of human beings as such; and what is reasonable is in accordance with human nature as such."[6] John Finnis pointed out that "for Aquinas, the way to discover what is morally right (virtue) and wrong (vice) is to ask, not what is in accordance with human nature, but what is reasonable."[7] The Late Scholastics also defined natural law as what our reason tells us about the nature of things.[8]

From this point of view, human good is in accord with reason; conversely, human evil lies outside the order of reasonableness. This can be seen in the paragraph that Aquinas appends to his discussion of reasonableness:

---

[6] St. Thomas Aquinas, *Summa,* I–II, qu. 71, art. 2, resp. The text in Latin reads, *"Et ideo id quod est contra ordinem rationis proprie est contra naturam hominis inquantum est homo; quod autem est secundum rationem est secundum naturam hominis inquantum est homo."*

[7] John Finnis, *Natural Law and Natural Rights* (Oxford: Clarendon Press, 1980), p. 36.

[8] Jose Mario Juan Cravero analyzes this definition in his *La Ley Natural en la Filosofía Económica de Fray Tomás de Mercado (d. 1575)*, Biblioteca del Pensamiento Económico Latinoamericano del Período Hispano (Bibleh), Consejo Nacional de Investigaciones Científicas y Técnicas (Conicet), Serie Ensayos y Conferencias, No. 2 (Buenos Aires: Facultad de Ciencias Sociales y Económicas de la Pontificia Universidad Católica Argentina Santa Maria de los Buenos Aires, 1983).

So human virtue, which makes good both the human person and his work, is in accordance with human nature just in so far as it is in accordance with reason; and vice is contrary to human nature just in so far as it is contrary to the order of reasonableness.[9]

To ascertain the reasonableness of something, one must examine cause-and-effect relationships, a process that calls for scientific research and study. For Aquinas, all knowledge of truth is a kind of *irridatio* and *participatio* of eternal law. All laws that can be regarded as knowledge (i.e., true laws) are natural laws (i.e., the participation of the eternal law in the rational creature).[10] For Luis de Molina, one of the most important Late Scholastics, what is naturally just derives from the nature of things (*natura rei*). It was easy for the Scholastics to proceed from the study of the nature of things, where they made use of all their analytical concepts, to the consideration of what is naturally just (*iustum naturale*).[11] In other words, their analytical judgments

---

[9] "*Unde virtus humana, quae hominem facit bonum, et opus ipsius bonum reddit, intantum est secundum naturam hominis inquantum convenit rationi; vitium autem intantum est contra naturam hominis inquantum est contra ordinem rationis.*" Aquinas, *Summa,* I–II, qu. 71, art. 2, resp.

[10] Aquinas, *Summa,* I–II, qu. 91, art. 2. Not all eternal truth can be understood by reason. Through theoretical (speculative) reason one can acquire the "knowledge of certain general principles but not proper knowledge of each single truth". *Summa,* I–II, qu. 91, art. 3. Natural law is a dictate of practical reason. "And so this is the first command of law, 'That good is to be sought and done and evil to be avoided'; all other precepts of the natural law are based upon this: so that whatever the practical reason naturally apprehends as man's good or evil belongs to the precepts of the natural law as something to be achieved." *Summa,* I–II, qu. 94, art. 2. The process of practical reason starts from certain principles and arrives at certain conclusions. Based on the nature of natural law, human reason must make more specific arrangements. *Summa,* I–II, qu. 91, art. 3. Natural law pertains to the sphere of practical reason.

[11] Luis de Molina, *De Iustitia et Iure* (Moguntiae, 1614), Tr. 1, dis. 4. The text in Latin reads "*Cuius obligatio oritur ex natura rei*". The late Joseph Schumpeter wrote that Luis de Molina "clearly identified natural law, on the one hand, with the dictates of reason (*ratio recta*), and with what is socially expedient or necessary (*expediens et necessarium*), on the other . . . he definitely married natural law to our rational diagnosis". *History of Economic Analysis* (Oxford: Oxford University Press, 1954), p. 109.

influenced their ethical pronouncements.[12] In fact, their main concerns were normative natural law and ethical judgments. With regard to money debasement, for instance, their principal objective was to determine if it was good or bad and for what reason. This meant that they first had to address other issues such as the nature of money debasement and its effects, an analytical question that is easily distinguishable from ethical issues. Since at times they employed the two concepts of natural law interchangeably, it is important to point out the difference between ethical and analytical judgments in their writings.

The Nature of Ethics

Ethics is a normative discipline that studies voluntary human conduct, including

> all actions, and also omissions, over which man exercises personal control, because he understands and wills these actions (and omissions) in relation to some end he has in view.[13]

Ethics may thus be defined as,

> The philosophical study of voluntary human action, with the purpose of determining what types of activity are good, right and to be done (or bad, wrong and not to be done) that man may live well.[14]

Man's actions are the subject of other disciplines as well: economics, sociology and psychology, for example. The primary interest in these fields, however, is not what man *ought* to do, but *how* he acts:

---

[12] The *New Catholic Encyclopedia* offers the following explanation: "A normative system presupposes an explanatory theory for analyzing economic phenomena; and the proponents of an explanatory natural law, rarely content to remain at the level of pure analysis, tend to elevate their conclusions into norms of ethics and canons of policy," s.v. "Natural Law in Economics", by L. C. Brown. The same author says "The rehabilitation of a normative natural law will require a better command of economic theory by its proponents." Ibid.

[13] Ibid.

[14] *New Catholic Encyclopedia*, s.v. "Ethics" by V. J. Bourke.

Such studies are non-normative. . . . In ancient and medieval thought, [economics and politics] were part of ethics; today they have become non-normative, and are regarded as outside the scope of ethics.[15]

From the ethical perspective, it is not enough to know what man does; it is important to know which of the things he does are good. The Schoolmen's primary intent was to study human action from an ethical standpoint.

The Nature of Economics

According to Carl Menger, economics is a theoretical *science* with the task of investigating and describing the general nature and general interconnection of economic phenomena.[16] His disciple, Ludwig von Mises, wrote that economics is the study of human action. As such, it

is a theoretical science and . . . abstains from any judgment of value. It is not its task to tell the people what ends they should aim at. It is a science of the means to be applied for the attainment of ends chosen, not, to be sure, a science of the choosing of ends.[17]

In his classical book on this subject, Lionel Robbins defined economics as "the science which studies human behaviour as a relationship between ends and scarce means which have alternative uses".[18] According to Paul Samuelson,

Economics is the study of how men and society choose, with or without the use of money, to employ *scarce* productive resources, which could have alternative uses, to produce various commodi-

---

[15] Ibid.

[16] Carl Menger, *Problems of Economics and Sociology* (Urbana, Ill.: University of Illinois Press, 1963), pp. 39, 210.

[17] Ludwig von Mises, *Human Action,* 2nd ed. (New Haven, Conn.: Yale University Press, 1959), p. 10.

[18] Lionel Robbins, *An Essay on the Nature and Significance of Economic Science* (London: Macmillan, 1952), p. 16.

ties over time and distribute them for consumption, now and in the future, among various people and groups in society.[19]

These definitions have something in common. They point out that economics is not a normative science. Rather, it is the study of the formal implications that can be deduced from the fact that human beings act purposively. It does not consider whether these actions are good or bad (an ethical question). Economic science is value free. It analyzes cause-and-effect relationships that, if true, are scientific. It is therefore inappropriate for the economist, as such, to make ethical judgments regarding these relationships. Only human acts can be judged morally.

Although it is difficult to conceive of a scientist who is not concerned with ethical questions, we can postulate the existence of non-normative sciences. Economics is one of these. The task of economic analysis is limited to explaining cause-and-effect relationships,

> it abstracts from the ethical character of human conduct, leaving to ethics the making of value judgments of a moral character. Economic analysis is concerned with how men *do* act, not with how they *should* act.[20]

The discoveries of *economic science* lead to the formulation of *economic policy,* which is the structuring of the economic order according to a legal framework. This involves human action. According to Carl Menger, economic policy is "the science of the basic principles for suitable advancement (appropriate to conditions) of 'national economy' on the part of the public authorities".[21] The definition of *suitable* will, perforce, involve value judgments. To this end, Lionel Robbins suggests that a theory of economic policy "must take its ultimate criterion from outside economics".[22] It is first necessary to establish

[19] Paul A. Samuelson, *Economics, An Introductory Analysis.* 7th ed. (New York: McGraw-Hill, 1967), p. 5.

[20] *New Catholic Encyclopedia,* s.v. "Economics and Ethics", by T. F. Divine.

[21] Menger, *Problems,* p. 211.

[22] Lionel Robbins, *The Theory of Economic Policy in English Classical Political Economy* (London: Macmillan, 1952), pp. 176–177.

the moral values which will, in turn, determine the goals of economic policy.

On the other hand, economic policy can be regarded as a tool. As such it is value free. Tools and technologies do not teach us what is.

> Their problem is rather to determine the basic principles by which, according to the diversity of conditions, efforts of a definite kind can be most suitably pursued. They teach us what the conditions are *supposed* to be for definite human aims to be achieved. Technologies of this kind in the field of economy are *economic policy* and the *science of finance.* [23]

Economic policy is thus involved with the selection of economic goals (which is value oriented) and the implementation of these goals. It is possible to distinguish, without making value judgments, between those policies that are more likely to produce the desired ends and those that seem less fortuitous. Applied economic policy can be judged morally, since it is human action that proposes and implements legislation.

Economic doctrine (i.e., authoritative teaching of normative and positive economics) will influence goal selection. Since it deals with what the economic order should be, it can also be value oriented. For this reason there is a closer link between this branch of economics and ethics. Ethics exert a direct influence on economic doctrine. Be it explicitly or implicitly, every doctrine has a set of values attached to it.

Economic ethics, the consideration of whether human economic acts are good or evil, is also essentially a normative discipline. Ludwig von Mises is quoted as saying:

> An ethical standard is judging various modes of conduct from the point of view of a scale of values which derives from divine commandments, or from that which is in the soul of everyone. The realm of ethics is not something which is outside of that of economic action. You cannot deal with ethical problems apart from economic ones and vice versa. [24]

---

[23] Menger, *Problems,* p. 38.

[24] Margit von Mises, *My Years with Ludwig von Mises* (New Rochelle, N.Y.: Arlington House, 1976), p. 134.

Not only are value judgments implicit in economic ethics, they are its essence. Such evaluations must embrace three realms: the doctrines that influence economic policy, the policy itself and the tools it employs. Economic ethics thus encompasses and is informed by many areas of scientific and philosophical thought.

Economists should be very careful when crossing the border into ethics. One can agree with T. F. Divine that as a

> specialist in his own area of economic analysis, the economist could hardly be expected to qualify also as an expert in philosophy, religion, law, politics, psychology, aesthetics, etc.; and unless so qualified, he would hardly be competent to make value judgments in those spheres.[25]

The same applies to moralists wishing to make value judgments concerning economic matters without specialized training in the subject.

The Influence of Ethics on Economics

Ethical evaluations influence and are influenced by economic judgments. In a society where people consider the possession of riches and the process of capital accumulation to be praiseworthy (doctrine), the legal treatment of profits (policy) will tend to be different than in those societies where they are viewed with contempt. The same can be said of many other moral points of view.

Historically, ethical judgments have influenced the development of economic science. The selection of a topic and of research tools takes place within the limits imposed on inquiry by moral values. Since Canon Law expressly condemned the charging of interest, many Medieval scholars avoided scientific consideration of the subject. The same happened in other scientific fields. Ethical condemnation of dissection, for example, prohibited anatomical studies that later became a significant factor in medical science. It is important to note, however,

[25] *New Catholic Encyclopedia,* s.v. "Economics and Ethics", by T. F. Divine, p. 83.

that while ethical considerations may either promote or hinder scientific development, they have no impact on underlying truths. No ethical judgment can invalidate an economic law.

Economic science describes "what is". Ethics describes "what ought to be". The difference between what is and what ought to be, between facts and values, underlies the entire domain of normative ethics. Although facts are not values, they are, nevertheless, related to values. Any discussion of the problems of ethics must consider this interrelationship.[26]

The more correct our economic analysis is, the greater the possibility of making correct moral economic judgments.[27] This is not to say that the task of an economist is limited to determining "what ought to be" on the basis of "what is". He must consider the myriad implications of both facts and values.

As moralists, the Late Scholastics devoted their major efforts to the discussion of what is just and good. With their attention focused on the broad spectrum of human action, it was natural for them to study economic issues. Such questions as the right to charge interest, the propriety of profits, the ethics of monetary intervention, the justice of taxes, were, in their view, not only appropriate but essential topics of discussion. They recognized the need to study all aspects of the phenomena, i.e., interest, profits, taxes, etc., before making ethical valuations. They knew that when properly conducted, such study is value free.

The fact that the Late Scholastics operated from a world view in which moral issues permeated every aspect of human life does not mean that their study lacked objectivity. They employed the tools of reason and deduction to describe economic processes. The purpose of such study (i.e., to make ethical judgments) does not invalidate the procedures or the conclusions. Rather than taking into account the

[26] See for example, Julius Kovesi, "Against the Ritual of 'Is' and 'Ought' ", *Midwestern Studies in Philosophy* 3 (1978): pp. 5–16; Ralph McInerny "Naturalism and Thomistic Ethics", *The Thomist* 40 (April, 1976): pp. 222–242.

[27] Paul W. Taylor, *Problems of Moral Philosophy: An Introduction to Ethics* (Belmont, Calif.: Dickenson, 1967), p. 366.

purposes behind a theory, we must analyze the latter to see if it is correct.

Although research in such fields as political science, economics and political economy may not alter the foundations of ethics (since "The complete justification of any value judgment goes beyond the statement of relevant facts about the object being judged"),[28] it can help to resolve moral issues that appear intractable or at least resistent to resolution by moral argument alone. Although economic analysis can influence ethical judgments, it cannot alter fundamental moral principles. For example, it may change the attitude people have toward inflation, but it cannot modify the principle that stealing is wrong.[29]

The Importance of Natural-Law Theories

The Late Scholastics derived their ethical approach from the Thomist concept of the interrelatedness of natural law, ethics and economics. From the Medieval perspective, the application of *jus* naturalism to social science did no more than posit the existence of a natural order. In their efforts to understand the "natural economic order", it was logical for them to employ economic reasoning.[30]

To believe in natural laws is to believe in natural order. Even the critics of the natural-law approach find positive factors in

---

[28] Ibid.

[29] Tom L. Beauchamp offers an interesting analysis of this issue in "The Foundations of Ethics and the Foundations of Science", to be found in *Knowing and Valuing: The Search for Common Roots,* ed. H. T. Engelhardt, Jr., and D. Callahan, vol. 4 (New York: Hastings Center, Institute of Society, Ethics and the Life Sciences, 1980), pp. 260–269.

[30] Joseph A. Schumpeter includes a fine analysis of this topic in his *History of Economic Analysis* (New York: Oxford University Press, 1954), pp. 110–113.

it. Ludwig von Mises[31] recognized three important contributions:

    a. Belief in the existence of a natural order.

    b. The importance of human reason as the only means of understanding the natural order.

    c. The method of judging the goodness of an action by its effects (which led eventually to a special type of utilitarianism).

As noted, every scientific law that is a true statement is a natural law, something that human beings can understand but cannot alter. It is always useful for human beings to understand cause-and-effect relationships. Karl Popper wrote that the knowledge of natural laws can be used "for technical purposes . . . and . . . we may get into trouble by not knowing them, or by ignoring them".[32] Although the knowledge of the natural order *may* be aided by revelation, reason must *always* be employed in the discovery of such knowledge.

In this sense, we can understand why it was logical for the Late Scholastics to use utilitarian arguments to prove that something was *natural.* The impact of natural law on Late-Scholastic analysis of economics is diagrammed in Figure 2. Natural law, in both analytical and normative form, derives from eternal law. The former influences (but does not predetermine) ethical reasoning. Both analytical and

---

[31] "It would be a serious blunder to ignore the fact that all the varieties of the doctrine contained a sound idea which could neither be compromised by connection with untenable vagaries nor discredited by any criticism. Long before the Classical economists discovered that a regularity in the sequence of phenomena prevails in the field of human action, the champions of natural law were dimly aware of this inescapable fact. From the bewildering diversity of doctrines presented under the rubric of natural law there finally emerged a set of theorems which no caviling can ever invalidate. There is first the idea that a nature-given order of things exists to which man must adjust his actions if he wants to succeed. Second: the only means available to man for the cognizance of this order is thinking and reasoning, and no existing social institution is exempt from being examined and appraised by discursive reasoning. Third: there is no standard available for appraising any mode of action either of individuals or of groups of individuals but that of the effects produced by such action. Carried to its ultimate logical consequences, the idea of natural law led eventually to rationalism and utilitarianism." Von Mises, *Theory and History* (New Haven, Conn.: Yale University Press, 1957), pp. 44–45.

[32] Popper, *The Open Society,* p. 59.

normative natural law influence economic policy and economic doctrines, as well as economic ethics.

Figure 2.

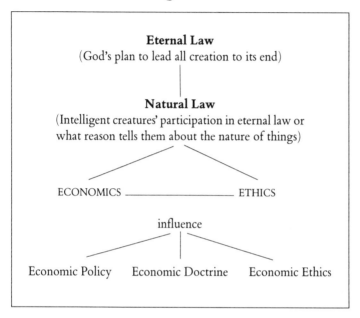

This understanding of nature and human action exerted a significant influence on the foundations and premises of modern economic thought. As Joseph Schumpeter wrote,

> The doctrine of Natural Law which in the sixteenth century grew into an independent discipline is of still greater importance to us. It is very difficult to give an adequate idea of the extent of scientific progress made within this framework.[33]

---

[33] Joseph A. Schumpeter, *Economic Doctrine and Method* (New York: Oxford University Press, 1954), pp. 19–20.

PART TWO

THE LATE–SCHOLASTIC
CONTRIBUTIONS TO ECONOMICS

3

PRIVATE PROPERTY

One day, as St. Francis was travelling through a city, a demon-possessed person appeared in front of him and asked: "What is the worst sin in the world?" St. Francis answered that homicide was the worst. But the demon replied that there was one sin still worse than homicide. St. Francis then commanded: "By God's virtue, tell me which sin is worse than homicide!" And the devil answered that having goods that belong to someone else is a sin worse than homicide because it is this sin which sends more people to Hell than any other.[1]

Continuing the Thomistic tradition, the Late Scholastics ascribed great importance to the justification of private property, stating that it derives from both eternal and natural law. Some of the early Scholastic authors had argued that things should be owned in common and had condemned those who possessed riches. The Late Scholastics rejected this condemnation, employing scriptural arguments and analysis of human action to prove their point.

Those who opposed private property often quoted the passage describing the rich young man (Luke 18:18–25). A member of a leading family approached Jesus and asked him,

"Good Master, what have I to do to inherit eternal life?" Jesus said to him, "Why do you call me good? No one is good but God alone. You know the commandments: You must not commit adultery; You must not kill; You must not steal; You must not bring false witness; Honour your father and mother." He replied, "I have kept all these from my earliest days till now." And when Jesus heard this he said, "There is still one thing you lack. Sell all that you own and distribute the money to the poor, and you will have treasure in heaven;

[1] Story told by St. Bernardino of Siena in Sermon XXVII of *"De Amore Irratio"*, *Opera Omnia* (Venice, 1591).

then come, follow me." But when he heard this he was filled with sadness, for he was very rich.

Jesus looked at him and said, "How hard it is for those who have riches to make their way into the kingdom of God! Yes, it is easier for a camel to pass through the eye of a needle than for a rich man to enter the kingdom of God."[2]

Although many authors think that Jesus was condemning the possession of riches, the Late Scholastics, indicated that this was not the correct interpretation. Citing Luke 14:26, where Jesus says, "If any man come to me without hating his father, mother, wife, children, brothers, sisters, yes and his own life too, he cannot be my disciple," the Scholastics pointed out that this passage does not enjoin Christians to hate their fathers. Such doctrine would contradict the Fourth Commandment. Thomist and Scholastic interpretation of this passage is that entrance to the kingdom of Heaven is denied to anyone who values things more than God.[3] In Matthew's Gospel (10:37), the same passage reads: "Anyone who prefers father or mother to me is not worthy of me. Anyone who prefers son or daughter to me is not worthy of me." It would be a violation of the natural order to value a created thing above its creator, as did the young

---

[2] Scriptural references are from the *Jerusalem Bible.*

[3] St. Thomas Aquinas wrote, "The rich man in question was criticized for thinking that external goods were his absolutely as if he had not first received them from another, namely God", *Summa Theologica* (London: Blackfriars, 1975), II–II, qu. 66, art. 1, resp. 2.

ruler who pursued riches as his ultimate goal.[4] As is indicated in Luke (12:29–31):

> you must not set your heart on things to eat and things to drink; nor must you worry. It is the pagans of this world who set their hearts on all these things. Your father well knows you need them. No; set your hearts on his kingdom, and these other things will be given you as well.

With regard to the question of riches, it is helpful to note that many people close to Jesus were quite wealthy for their times. Joseph seems to have had his own business and perhaps a donkey; Peter owned a fishing boat, and Matthew was a tax collector. Jesus praised the rich man Zaccheus.[5] It was the wealthy Joseph of Arimathea who kept faith even when the Apostles were beset by doubt (Mt 27:57). Jesus does not condemn the possession of riches but, rather, disordered attachment to them.[6]

Those who opposed private property also cited Acts 2:44–47:

> The faithful all lived together and owned everything in common; they sold their goods and possessions and shared out the proceeds among themselves according to what each one needed.

---

[4] Most of the Late Scholastics cited the same passages. Henrique de Villalobos, for example, wrote: "*Y no obsta contra la conclusion lo que dixo Christo: q. Nisi quis renunciaverit omnibus qui possidet, non potest meus esse discipulus: porque en el mismo capitulo tambien dize:* Si quis venit ad me, & non odit patrem, & matrem &c. *Y es llano, que no tiene obligación el hombre de aborrecer a su padre, y madre, pues ay precepto de lo contrario. Y assi el sentido destos dos lugares, es que se deven dexar estas cosas, quando fuere estorvo para la vida eterna.*" *Summa de la Theologia Moral y Canónica* (Barcelona, 1632), p. 140. Pedro de Aragón said that Christ's words should not be taken as a commandment but as advice and that those who possess riches can achieve eternal life. *De Iustitia et Iure* (Lyon, 1596), p. 109. After discussing the topic in similar terms, Domingo de Bañez states that Christ is condemning "distorted and inordinate love" (*amore pravo & inordinato*), *De Iustitia et Iure Decisiones* (Salamanca, 1594), p. 131.

[5] Miguel Salón, *Commentariorum in Disputationem de Iustitia Quam Habet D. Tho. Secunda Sectione Secundae partis suae Summa Theologicae* (Valencia, 1591), p. 389.

[6] Juan de Medina is also very clear about this topic, stating that to achieve salvation one must renounce affection for property but not its possession (*renunciatione rerum quoad affectum, & mentis preparationem, non quoad effectum*). *De Contractibus* (Salamanca, 1550), p. 2.

They went as a body to the Temple every day but met in their houses for the breaking of bread; they shared their food gladly and generously; they praised God and were looked up to by everyone.

As did St. Thomas,[7] the Late Scholastics recalled St. Augustine's condemnation of the teachings of the so-called "Apostolics". They declared that it was heresy to say that those who have property cannot enter the kingdom of heaven. Lessio noted that there are many passages in the Scriptures that state that possession is not a sin.[8] Miguel Salón invoked the authority of St. Augustine in this regard.[9] Juan de Medina also quoted St. Augustine and added that although some of the Apostles had property, Jesus did not ask them to renounce it. Medina further noted that natural law neither mandates nor prohibits the division of goods.[10]

Pedro de Aragón explained that if we suppose that it is better for certain men (for example, members of religious orders) to possess goods in common, it does not follow that the same can be said for all

---

[7] St. Thomas Aquinas quotes St. Augustine in his *Summa,* II–II, Q. 66, art. 2, resp.: "Augustine says: *The people styled apostolic are those who arrogantly claimed this title for themselves because they refused to admit married folk or property owners to their fellowship, arguing from the model of the many monks and clerics in the Catholic Church* (*De Haeresibus* 40). But such people are heretics because they cut themselves off from the Church by alleging that those who, unlike themselves, marry and own property have no hope for salvation."

[8] Leonardo Lessio, *De Iustitia et Iure* (Antwerp, 1626), p. 41: the Latin text reads: *"Post peccatum haec dominiorum divisio non solum fuit licita, sed etiam salutaris generi humano. Quod licita fuerit, est certo tenendum. Nam ex multis Scripturae locis constat,* licite aliquid tamquam proprium possideri: *contrarium est heresis quorumdam, qui vocat sunt Apostolici, ut refert D. Aug. haeresi 40. & Epiphanius haeresi 61. qui asserebant hominem non posse salvari, nisi vineret instar Apostolorum, nudus ab omni divitiarum proprietate."*

[9] Salón, *Commentariorum,* p. 389; the text in Latin reads: *"Haec est de fide. Ita. D. Aug. locis citatis, maxime lib. de haeresibus cap. 40. ubi illos haereticos Apostolicos hoc nomine vocat haereticos, quia contra fidem & doctrinam Ecclesie Catholica & Apostolorum damnarent rerum divisionem, & propria ac privata dominia, quae fideles habent in suas res."*

[10] Medina, *De Contractibus,* p. 140; the Spanish text reads: *"Y en el testamento nuevo, aunque los Apóstoles tenian algo, no se los mando Christo dexar. Y no es esto contrario al derecho natural, por el qual las cosas son comunes, que esto se ha de entender, que no estan divididas de derecho natural."*

human beings in general.[11] By the same token, one might conclude that since priests must remain celibate, no one should marry.

According to both Medina and Aragón, the condemnation of Ananias (for pretending to give up all his wealth) does not prove that riches are evil. Ananias' sin was lying to the Holy Spirit.[12] To further prove his point, Medina quoted Psalm 62: "Though riches may increase, keep your heart detached."[13] Villalobos quoted Proverbs 10:22: "The blessing of Yahweh is what brings riches, to this hand toil has nothing to add."[14]

In addition to scriptural references, the Medieval Schoolmen employed logic and reasoning. They posited the convenience of private property for the development of mankind. The Doctors offered utilitarian arguments to show that goods that are privately owned are better used than commonly owned goods. This explanation offers a budding theory of economic development: the division of goods and their ultimate possession by private individuals facilitates increased production.

Domingo de Soto criticized common ownership from an Aristote-

---

[11] Aragón, *De Iustitia,* pp. 110–111; the Latin text reads: *"Hoc supposito dico, quod quanuis simpliciter & per se loquendo, melius sit in communi vivere, quam res privatum possidere; imo religiosis, & aliis, qui Deo vacare volunt melius est sic vivere, quam alio modo: tamen universo generi humano melio est possessio rerum in particulari, propter rationes iam dictas. Unde ad argumentum respondetur concessa maiori, atq; minori, negando consequentiam, si loquamur de convenientia respectu totius generis humani."*

[12] Medina, *De Contractibus,* p. 2; Aragón, *De Iustitia,* p. 111.

[13] *"Divitie si affluant, nolite cor apponere."* Medina, ibid.

[14] *"Benedictio Dei facit divites."* Henrique de Villalobos, *Summa* de la Theologia Moral y Canónica (Barcelona, 1632), p. 140.

lian and Thomist perspective.[15] Stating that it is impossible to achieve abundance in a common property system, he suggested three possible arrangements: (a) land that is privately owned while its produce is commonly shared, (b) commonly owned land whose produce is privately enjoyed and (c) common possession of both the land and its fruits. Soto admitted that each of these systems has its drawbacks. In the first case, disputes will arise.

> The rewards of labor will be unequal. Those who own more land will have to work more, while the fruits of their labor will be distributed to all equally according to need. They will resent receiving less for working more.[16]

With common ownership of land involving private ownership of fruits, "everyone will expect the others to do the work". Since people's love for their own goods is strong, "the distribution of goods will cause great envy".[17] Similar problems would arise if both the land and its fruits were commonly owned:

> Each worker will try to appropriate as many goods as possible, and given the way human beings desire riches, everyone will behave in

[15] Soto's and many Scholastic writers' analyses can be regarded as a development of Thomist theories. St. Thomas Aquinas, also from an Aristotelian perspective, wrote that private property is necessary for human life for three reasons: "First, because each person takes more trouble to care for something that is his sole responsibility than what is held in common or by many—for in such a case each individual shirks the work and leaves the responsibility to somebody else, which is what happens when too many officials are involved. Second, because human affairs are more efficiently organized if each person has his own responsibility to discharge; there would be chaos if everybody cared for everything. Third, because men live together in greater peace where everyone is content with his task [sic] (*re sua contentus est*). We do, in fact, notice that quarrels often break out amongst men who hold things in common without distinction." (*Inter eos qui communiter et ex indiviso aliquid possident frequentius jurgia oriuntur*). It is important to note that in this edition the phrase *"re sua contentus est"* is translated "everyone is content with his *task*". A more precise version would read "everyone is content with his *things*". In this passage St. Thomas stated that satisfaction may be derived from ownership of private property. *Summa*, II–II, qu. 66, art. 2, resp.

[16] Domingo de Soto, *De Iustitia et Iure* (Madrid: IEP, 1968), bk. IV, qu. 3, fol. 105–106.

[17] Ibid.

the same fashion. The peace, tranquility and friendship sought by
the philosophers will thus inevitably be subverted.[18]

When goods are commonly owned, the orderly society and a peaceful division of labor are impossible. Since no one will be willing
to accept the more dangerous jobs, society will forfeit tranquility.

In addition to their economic arguments in favor of private property,
the Late Scholastics also cited moral reasons. Soto wrote that in a
context of commonly owned goods, the virtue of liberality would
disappear, since "those who own nothing cannot be liberal".[19] The
virtue of hospitality would also become impossible, since no one
would own a home. Soto then quoted St. Augustine's dictum that it
was heresy to state that it is sinful to own property. He noted that
even the clergy may have property of their own. Indeed, the Council
of Constance (1414–1418) censored John Hus for opposing this
principle.[20] In response to the objection that private property has not
resolved the disputes and evils that occur in society, Soto explained
that for a law to be just, "it is not required that all its ends should
be accomplished". He further stated that "there is no law which can
prevent men from using their freedom in disorderly fashion".[21]
Although the institution of private property promotes peace and
equality, it cannot guarantee the abolition of evil.

Tomás de Mercado also acknowledged the existence of self-interest
and the greater care that humans generally exercise in relation to
their own property. He pointed out that common ownership is counter-
productive

> because people love most those things that belong to them. If I love
> God, it is *my* God, Creator and Saviour whom I love. If I love him
> who engendered me, it is *my* father whom I love. If a father loves his
> children, it is because they are *his*. If a wife loves her husband it is

---

[18] Ibid. Domingo de Soto is speaking of the philosophers such as Plato and
even Aristotle who favored some sort of common ownership.

[19] Ibid.

[20] Ibid.

[21] Ibid.

because he *belongs* to *her* and vice versa. . . . And if I love a friend it is *my* friend or *my* parent or *my* neighbor. If I desire the common good, it is for the benefit of *my* religion or *my* country or *my* republic. Love always involves the word *"mine"* and the concept of property is basic to love's nature and essence.[22]

Due to original sin, there is so much covetousness that "the whole world is insufficient for one person, much less for everyone".[23] Realizing that economic goods are scarce, Mercado espoused private property as an efficient method of reducing—if not overcoming—scarcity.

We cannot find a person who does not favor his own interests or who does not prefer to furnish his home rather than that of the republic. We can see that privately owned property flourishes, while city- and council-owned property suffers from inadequate care and worse management. In this regard, Aristotle states that the pleasure a man feels while working at his own business is inevitable. It is not easy to explain how important it is for man to know that he is the owner of the thing he produces. On the other hand, people treat common enterprises with great indifference. . . . After man's loss of innocence, it becomes necessary for each individual to share in the things of this world, in real estate or moveable riches. . . . If universal love won't induce people to take care of things, private interest will. Hence, privately owned goods will multiply. Had they remained in common possession, the opposite would be true.[24]

Juan de Mariana also referred to the relationship between self-interest and the careful use of economic goods. He was not entirely in favor of those who questioned:

Who is going to despoil man of this condition or instinct unless he desires to destroy all the foundations of individual well being? Is there anything more injudicious than to act against our own interests,

---

[22] Tomás de Mercado, *Summa de Tratos y Contratos* (Seville, 1571), bk. II, chap. II, fol. 18–19. [Italics mine.]
[23] Ibid., fol. 19.
[24] Ibid.

as justice not infrequently demands, in order to serve the interests of another people?[25]

He did, however, recognize that self-interest is a natural thing in animate beings. "If the exchange of goods were abolished", he added, "society would be impossible, and we would all live in distress and anguish. We would not have faith in our children nor would children trust their parents."[26] Society exists, then, because man is not self-sufficient. "Scarcity can be overcome through mutual exchange of those items owned in abundance by one party or the other."[27] He then admonished the authorities to keep in mind the fact that "nothing induces action more than one own's utility, be the man a prince or a citizen", and that the prince should not trust "in alliances and friendships where no profit can be expected".[28] With a high degree of self-criticism, he cited the example of the poor use the Jesuits made of the things they owned in common:

> We are too extravagant. Our cassocks are made of black woolen cloth and we are supplied everything in common, from the littlest to the biggest items: papers, ink, books and our provisions for journeys [*viaticum*]. Certainly it is natural for people to spend much more when they are supplied in common than when they have to obtain things on their own. The extent of our common expenses is unbelievable.[29]

Bartolome de Albornoz noted that even the priests indulged in economic abuses when their goods were handled in common rather than privately. When things belong to a priest, fraud is unlikely

> because, since the goods belong to a person, they have an owner who can be hurt, so he is going to guard against being fooled. This

---

[25] Juan de Mariana, *Del Rey y de la Institución Real,* in *Biblioteca de Autores Españoles,* Rivadeneyra, vol. 31 (Madrid: editions Atlas, 1950), p. 559.

[26] Ibid., p. 560.

[27] Ibid.

[28] Ibid., p. 567.

[29] Mariana, *Discurso de las Cosas de la Compañia,* in *Biblioteca de Autores Españoles,* vol. 31, p. 604; in Spanish it reads, *"se gasta lo que no se puede creer".*

does not occur in the Church workshop since it is not the property of a private citizen who is personally interested in it. The popular saying "a donkey owned by many wolves is soon eaten" derives from this reasoning.[30]

Albornóz further reported that the people in charge of the church workshop are such butchers that they kill the cow (losing all the future milk, butter, cheese and calves), sacrificing a hundred pounds of meat to earn a few cents. In his example, the officials in charge of the workshop declare that the Church needs a chalice or a paten and order the butler to make it. "If the butler states honestly that the workshop is out of money or in debt, he is excommunicated."[31]

Luis de Molina included many passages favoring private property in his *De Iustitia et Iure*. If things were held in common, he said, they would be poorly cultivated and administrated. Scarcity would ensue, and men would fight each other for the use and consumption of goods. The powerful would inevitably exploit the weak. No one would be interested in serving the public good, and no one would agree to work in those jobs that require greater effort.[32] According to Molina, private property may have existed even before original sin, since in that state, men could agree by common consent to divide the goods of the earth.[33] The commandment "thou shalt not steal" implies that the division of goods does not pervert natural law.[34] All the Late Scholastic authors granted considerable importance to the moral use of goods that private property allows. "Alms should be given from

[30] Bartolomé de Albornóz, *Arte de los Contratos* (Valencia, 1573), p. 75.

[31] Ibid. Instead of buying from the cheapest suppliers, they buy from the most expensive ones.

[32] Luis de Molina, *De Iustitia et Iure* (Moguntiae, 1614), De Dominio, col. 100–101.

[33] The paragraph in Latin reads: *"Quod arbitror verum esse non solum in statu naturae lapse, sed etiam in statu naturae integrae potuissent namque homines in illo statu de comuni consensu dividere inter se et apropiare absque cuiusquam iniura res omnib. A deo concessas non secus ac in statu naturae lapsae iustissimis de causis effectum est."* Ibid.

[34] *"Imo praeceptum de non furando supponit rerum divisionem. Ergo rerum divisio non est contrarius naturale (alio quin ipso jure esset nulla) Quin potius approbata est in scripturis sacra."* Ibid., p. 102.

private goods and not from the common ones."[35] The virtues of charity, liberality, hospitality and generosity would all become impossible in a world without private property.

It is not surprising that these authors employed utilitarian arguments, especially since they preceded them with demonstrations that the division of goods is in accordance with natural law. For the Late Scholastics, however, the division of external things was a matter of *ius gentium,* which stems from different principles than the ones on which natural law is based.[36] Bañez stated that *natural law* consists of self-evident principles and the conclusions that necessarily derive from them. As we mentioned on page 28, he provided the example of the Golden Rule and its application to private property. From the principle of natural law, "Do unto others as you would have them do unto you", he arrived at the conclusion, "You must not steal". *Ius gentium,* on the other hand, may be defined as "the part of a legal system, whether international or national, that is derived from common customs prevailing among different people".[37] According to Bañez, *ius gentium* does not refer to self-evident principles or to the conclusions that necessarily derive from them. Nevertheless, it leads to conclusions that are so convenient and useful to human society that every nation must recognize them. Bañez provided two examples of positive human law (common laws): first, that the division of property is necessary for human society, and second, that property must be divided. He specified that these two ideas are not self-evident. Rather, they proceed from useful principles. "The farming of the fields", for instance, "is indispensable for the maintenance of human life and peace in the republic".[38] Such precepts do not arise from the Golden Rule but from the recognition that men are capable of evil.

---

[35] Francisco de Vitoria, *De Justitia,* edited by Beltrán de Heredia (Madrid: Publicaciones de la Asociación Francisco de Vitoria, 1934), II–II, qu. 66, art. 2, p. 324.

[36] Soto, *De Iustitia,* bk. IV, qu. III, fol. 105.

[37] *New Catholic Encyclopedia,* s.v. "Ius Gentium", by J. C. H. Wu, vol. VII, p. 774. The same author wrote that "*ius gentium* is positive common law, nearer in spirit to natural law than to any particular civil law, and for this reason may be described as a vehicle of the *ius naturale*". Ibid.

[38] Bañez, *De Iustitia et Iure Decisiones,* qu. 57, fol. 12.

> We know that the fields are not going to be efficiently tilled in common ownership and that there will not be peace in the republic, so we see that it is convenient to undertake the division of goods.[39]

According to Lessio, after original sin, the division of domains into private property is not only licit but also fruitful for mankind. He cited many scriptural passages as proof. In reference to the second point—that the division of property is useful for mankind—his arguments followed Aristotle's teachings. Without private property, he avowed, things will be poorly cared for, and peace between men will be impossible. Lessio pointed out this was the case for the family of Abraham and Lot: they were appeased only when the land was divided (Gen 13).[40]

After repeating similar arguments, Antonio de Escobar y Mendoza explained that nearly all people, except the most savage, have given their consent to the division of property because goods are better administered in private hands.[41]

In summary, Late Scholastic thought provides several arguments in favor of private property:

1. Private property helps to ensure justice. Evil exists because men are sinners. If goods were commonly owned, it would be the evil men "and even the thieves and misers"[42] who would profit most, since they would take more from the barn and put less into it. Good men, on the other hand, would contribute more and profit less. The fact that the most immoral people dominate society represents a harmful element and a distortion of natural order.

2. Private property is useful for the preservation of peace and harmony among men. Whenever goods are held in common, disputes are inevitable.

---

[39] Ibid.

[40] Lessio, *De Iustitia et Iure,* chap. 5, dub. II, pp. 41–42.

[41] Antonio de Escobar y Mendoza, *Universae Theologiae Moralis,* Tomi Quinti pars prima, Iustitia et Iure (Lyon, 1662), chap. III, p. 4.

[42] Vitoria, *De Justitia,* p. 325.

3. Privately owned productive goods are more fruitful because it is natural for men to take better care of what is theirs than of what belongs to everybody; hence the medieval proverb, "A donkey owned by many wolves is soon eaten".
4. Private property is convenient for maintaining order in society, and it promotes free social cooperation. If everything were held in common, people would refuse to perform the less pleasant jobs.
5. No man (not even a priest) can detach himself from temporal goods. Original sin brings with it the problem of scarcity, which is the source of economic problems (i.e., the difference between unlimited needs and limited resources).

Now we are so attached to these temporalities and we have so many needs that it is necessary for each person to have property, regardless of its size, and each should know that he must live from that and leave his neighbor's property for him to use.

This participation and division is so necessary because of our own weakness and misery. These principles must apply even to members of religious orders who choose poverty in a desire to imitate original innocence. The prelates of such orders must distribute vestments, books, papers and other items so that the priests will make good use of some and those in need can use the rest.[43]

Underground Property

St. Thomas[44] and many of his disciples discussed the subject of ownership in reference to things found both on the surface of the earth and underneath it. Their analyses and conclusions are important for contemporary economic policies because twentieth-century legislation in many countries provides for different treatments of "surface property" and "underground property". Pedro de Ledesma, following St. Antonino's reasoning, remarked that those things that have never had an owner "belong to the one who finds them, and the one who finds

---

[43] Mercado, *Summa,* fol. 18.
[44] Aquinas, *Summa,* II–II, qu. 66, art. 5, resp. 2.

them does not commit theft by keeping them".[45] According to Ledesma, the finder has a natural right to appropriate such goods. He also recognized that in many kingdoms there were laws that overrode this right.

Those things that at one time had a proprietor, such as treasures, may, in certain circumstances, belong to the one who found them. Sometimes the finder may not keep the treasure, as, for instance, when the owner's family knew where the treasure was hidden. Miguel Salón remarked that the nature of the circumstances can affect the question of ownership. A treasure may be found in no-man's-land or on private property. It may be found by chance or through industry and art. After distinguishing between the treasures left or hidden and then forever forgotten and those deliberately left in such places as burial sites, he concluded that the latter do not belong to the finder, but rather to the depositor or his successors. For this reason, Salón criticized the Spaniards who appropriated Aztec and Inca treasures, describing this as simple robbery and declaring that these treasures should be restored to their real owners. By natural right, however, any treasures found in no-man's-land belong to the finder.[46] Salón specified that the same rule applied when someone found a treasure on his own property.

When a treasure was found on another person's property, the Medieval Schoolmen drew different conclusions. If the discovery of a treasure on another person's land was by chance, Salón decreed that half of it belonged to the owner of the land and the other half to the finder. On the other hand, if the discovery of this treasure was due to hard work and diligence, then it should belong totally to the owner of the land. The Scholastics based these precepts on the fact that if someone invests both means and effort in searching for a treasure on another person's property, it could be presupposed that this person knew of its existence. As a punishment for concealing such knowl-

---

[45] Pedro de Ledesma, *Suma* (Antwerp, 1614), Tratado VIII, Justicia Conmutativa, p. 443.

[46] *"Si inveniatur in loco, qui ad nullius particulare dominum pertineat, totus est inventoris."* Salón, *Commentariorum,* col. 1298.

edge and for attempted fraud, the entire treasure should be awarded
to the owner of the land. If there is evidence of true ignorance on the
part of the finder, and if the effort was invested for a purpose other
than finding the treasure, proper ajudication of possession would
vary.[47]

The majority of the Thomist authors could easily prove that if
somebody bought a piece of land with a treasure buried in it, then
that person was the treasure's real owner, even in the case where the
seller did not know about the treasure. Their major scriptural argument was St. Matthew 13:44: "The kingdom of heaven is like treasure
hidden in a field which someone has found; he hides it again, goes off
happy, sells everything he owns and buys the field." Miguel Salón and
Pedro de Ledesma employed this argument.

If natural law says that a treasure belongs to its finder, either totally
(as when the treasure was found on one's property or in no-man's-
land) or partially, it is logical to conclude that everything placed by
nature under the earth's surface reasonably belongs to the owner of
the surface. The Scholastics cited the examples of metal and mineral
deposits, especially silver and gold. Salón stated explicitly that "the
minerals and gold and silver deposits, as well as any other metal in its
natural state, belong to the owner of the land and are for his benefit".[48]
More than a century later, the Late Scholastic author P. Gabriel Antoine
(1678–1743) judged that

> stones, coal, clay, sand, iron mines, lead, which are found under
> someone's land, belong to the owner of the land. In effect they are
> part of the land, for it does not consist solely of the surface alone,
> but of its entire depth all the way to the earth's center, and here is
> where we can find these fruits. And the same can be said of metal
> deposits.[49]

---

[47] *"Punire audaciam ac temeritatem eius qui sine licentia domini voluit laborare, & exercere suam industriam in agro alieno."* Ibid.

[48] *"Mineralia & venae auri, argenti & cuiusque metalli stando in iure naturae sunt domini fundi et in bonis ipsius."* Ibid., col. 1307.

[49] P. Gabriel Antoine, *Theologia Moralis Universa* (Cracovia, 1774), p. 369.

It is important to remember that nature places minerals in the land by natural processes. By definition, treasures are items that human beings place purposely and artificially in the land. The Late Scholastic authors recognized the rights of the finder and of the original owner. Once the principle of private ownership of buried treasure is accepted, it is easier to recognize private ownership of natural resources.

These judgments were common among the theologians who commented on St. Thomas. The fact that they generalized their advocacy of private property in reference to subsurface products did not prevent them from recognizing that through positive legislation, the government (in their case, the king) could appropriate part of the profit derived from the exploitation of "underground property". Indeed, they specifically pointed out the differences in this regard between one kingdom and another. While some argued that the usual percentage retained was the fifth part of the metal produced, others noted that in Castille the percentage was 66.7 (⅔). This tax was always charged *"deductis expensis"*, that is to say, after all the expenses of discovery, extraction and development had been deducted.[50]

In the same manner in which the Late Scholastics justified taxes on agricultural goods, they advocated taxes on subsoil products as well. For these authors, taxes represented a restriction on the use and domain of private property.[51] In its effort to protect all property and for the attainment of peace, harmony, order and development, the government appropriated a portion of such property. Unfortunately, the Schoolmen found that the laws of the kingdom very often disregard the teachings of natural law. Having first stated that "by natural law, the minerals belong to the lord of the place where they are found",[52] Pedro de Ledesma added that

> there is a law [in Spain] that says that the profit obtained from metals and from the ironmongers belongs to the king. . . . Another law says

---

[50] Molina, *De Iustitia,* bk. 1, dis. 54, col. 242.

[51] Soto, *De Iustitia,* bk. IV, qu. 5, fol. 110.

[52] Ledesma, *Summa,* Tratado VIII, de *Justicia Conmutativa,* p. 443.

that nobody without a license or privilege from the king is allowed to extract or seize metals.[53]

The Spanish colonial system later imposed these same regulations in many Latin American countries.

One of the authors who greatly influenced the Hispanic Scholastics, Sylvestre de Priero, argued that the law that awarded the prince all treasures found by others, even if the treasures were found in privately owned fields, was both violent and contrary to natural and common law. Sylvestre criticized Paludano's comment that according to tradition, all treasures belong to the prince, regardless of the place where they are found. Domingo de Soto pointed out that this tradition

> has not been introduced in any of the well-organized societies ... and so if it was enacted in any place, it was through force and against natural and civil law.[54]

For Soto, anyone who found gold or other metals under an ownerless plot of land had ownership rights to those minerals. For this reason, it was unjust for the prince to require a percentage payment from the person who found the treasure. This could only be natural if the metal was found in a property belonging to the prince. The only exception Soto could find was in a case of grave public need, but even then he declared this an insufficient reason. Yet for metals, Domingo de Soto accepted a 20 percent tax, or what was called the "metallic fifth".[55]

Ownership and Use of Property

Quoting Conradus Summenhart, Francisco de Vitoria defined domain (*dominium*) as the faculty to use a thing according to reasonably established laws. People can use things although they are not the owners. In this sense, domain and use are distinct. Whenever man has perfect domain over a good, he can use this good as he pleases, even to

[53] Ibid., p. 454.
[54] Soto, *De Iustitia,* bk. V, qu. III, fol. 151.
[55] Ibid.

the extent of destroying it. As Villalobos pointed out, "Domain has to do with the substance of the thing; and so, the one who owns it can sell it, transfer it and if he wants, destroy it".[56] Use is the faculty of utilizing the thing regardless of who the owner is, as when one uses a neighbor's horse or clothing. Soto specified that the purpose of domain is the use of the thing. Indeed, the Late Scholastics argued that things are better used when they are held in private ownership than when they are held in common. When the Schoolmen said that things were better *used,* they were speaking of social, political, economical and, above all, *moral use.*

Diego de Covarrubias stated that everything that grows or that could be productive in a plot of land should belong to the owner of the land. This applies when the good will be very useful for the community as well as when it is there due to nature and not due to the labor and art of the owner.[57] According to Covarrubias, trees that produce medicinal fruits deserve high prices and great esteem, but it is false to conclude that, therefore, the owner has no right to prevent other people from using his goods.[58] Furthermore, the owner can modify or reduce the vegetation on his land. Covarrubias found nothing to grant common-property status to the plants and herbs growing on private property.

Among the uses of property, *transfers* of domain are essential for economics. Exchanges are, in essence, a transfer of domain. Domingo de Soto acknowledged that "there is nothing so much in agreement with natural justice as to enact the will of a man who wishes to transfer the domain [property] of his goods."[59] "Any person has the natural right to donate or transfer the things he legally owns in any way he wants." Soto added that if man can be a property owner

---

[56] Villalobos, *Summa,* p. 126.

[57] *"Quicquid nascitur in agro privato, etiam absque labore & industria domini, ad ipsum omnium pertinet."* Covarrubias y Leiva, *Opera Omnia,* chap. 37, p. 274.

[58] Ibid., p. 276.

[59] Soto, *De Iustitia,* bk. IV, qu. V, fol. 110.

because he has free-will, by this same free-will he can transfer his domain to anyone else.[60]

As all things have been created for man, he may use them as he pleases. Moreover, the ownership of something consists of the faculty and the right to use that thing in every way permitted by law, such as donating, transfering, selling or consuming it in any manner. Despite this natural right, however, Soto declared that the law may restrain the will of the owner and even deprive him of his good against his will. Although man is a social being and he will therefore find it advantageous to live in society, the republic needs an authority, and the main function of public authority is to defend the republic and to administer justice. To fulfill its duty, authority has to supervise the use that young people make of their goods until they reach the age of full reason. Second, Soto declared that some goods must be used to support authority (in the form of taxes). Third, authority has the duty to punish crimes. One form of punishment is depriving the guilty party of his goods. Other restrictions on the use of property refer to the use of ecclesiastical goods.

The fact that ownership is not exactly the use of a thing does not permit the conclusion that the domain of goods should be private and that their use should be common. This would contradict Late-Scholastic arguments in favor of private property. The Medieval Schoolmen favored private property becaused they deemed it better used and, therefore, more contributory to the welfare of all mankind.[61]

---

[60] "*Si ergo per voluntatem constituitur dominus, per eandem potest dominium ab se quodcunque abdicare.*" Ibid.

[61] See Raymond De Roover's study, *San Bernardino of Siena and Sant' Antonino of Florence: The Two Great Economic Thinkers of the Middle Ages* (Cambridge, Mass.: Kress Library, 1967), pp. 8–9.

4

PUBLIC FINANCE

Many people would like to expand the power of kings, increasing it beyond the limits of reason and law; some suggest this to win the king's favor and to increase their wealth (the courts and palaces are full of these dangerous people) . . . others because they think that this is the way to royal greatness and increased magnificence, i.e., the basis of public and individual welfare. But they are mistaken because power, like virtue, has its limits and degrees, and when they are surpassed, not only is it not strengthened, it is weakened and diminished. And as important authors say, power is not like money, the more one has the richer one is; it is like food for the stomach: too much or too little can weaken you. It is known that when kings expand their power over their boundaries, their rule degenerates into tyranny, which is not only evil but weak and short-lived as well, because its very citizens are its enemies and there is no effective weapon or force against their indignation.[1]

The Nature and Forms of Government

Believing that people's understanding of their government's function directly influences their opinions concerning the legitimacy and extent of public spending, the Late Scholastics addressed the issue of political structure. For Juan de Mariana, as well as for many other Schoolmen, the most important thing in politics was not the system but the rights and the conditions that the people of a certain society could enjoy:

---

[1] Juan de Mariana, *Tratado sobre la Moneda de Vellón,* in *Biblioteca de Autores Españoles,* Rivadeneyra, vol. 31 (Madrid: Editions Atlas, 1950), p. 578.

Politicians usually ask which is the best form of government. But for me this is secondary because I have seen states flourish under a republican rule as well as with a monarch.[2]

It seems that, at least for Mariana, the theory of subjective utility could also be applied to the analysis of political systems:

It happens in everything—in clothing, in shoes, in homes and in many other things—that even the best and the most elegant please some and do not please others. I think that the same thing can happen with different forms of government. Just because one form has advantages over all the rest, it does not have to be accepted by people used to different systems and customs.[3]

Mariana determined that the "Republic" was "properly named because all citizens participate in the government according to their rank and merit".[4] In "democracy", he stipulated, the honors and positions of the state are bestowed without reference to merit or social class, "something really against common sense because it attempts to equalize what nature or a superior and irresistible force made unequal". According to Mariana, society existed before power.

Only after society had been constituted could men have thought of creating power. This fact in itself is sufficient to prove that rulers exist for the people's benefit and not vice versa. . . . This can be confirmed and verified by our personal cry for liberty, a liberty which was first diminished when one man took up the sceptre of law or exercised the force of his sword over others.[5]

Such limitation of liberty is onerous but necessary, and it must spring from the people's will: "If, for our welfare, we need someone to govern us, we are the ones who must grant him the power, rather

---

[2] Mariana, *Biblioteca de Autores Españoles,* vol. 30, pp. XXVI–XXVII.

[3] Mariana, *Del Rey,* p. 471.

[4] Ibid., p. 477. (The word *republic* comes from the Latin, *res* = thing; *publica* = public).

[5] Mariana, *Biblioteca de Autores Españoles,* vol. 30, Discurso Preliminar, p. XXVII.

than him imposing it upon us with his sword."[6] Since government's main purpose is to adopt measures for attaining peace, it is perfectly consistent to conclude that one of the main functions of the state is to protect private property as a means of attaining peace.

Mariana was a harsh critic of several notoriously successful rulers. He declared that Cyrus, Alexander and Caesar

> were kings, but not legitimate ones. Instead of taming the tyrannical monster and eradicating vices . . . they applied the art of robbery. It is ironic that even today, people sing their praises.[7]

In the beginning, tyrants are soft and smiling, but once their power is well established, "their sole intent becomes to demolish and offend". "The rich and the good" become their prime victims. Like doctors who use the healing arts to try to expel bad viruses from the body, tyrants "work to expel from the republic those who can contribute most to its brightness and its future".[8]

> They drain individual treasures. Every day they impose new taxes. They plant the seeds of disruption among the citizens. They engage in one war after another. They put into practice every possible method to avoid rebellion against their cruel tyranny. *They construct large, monstruous monuments, but at the cost of the riches and over the protests of their subjects. Do you think, by chance, that the pyramids in Egypt and the underground caves in Olympus of Thesalia had a different origin?*[9]

According to Mariana, the king is not the lord of private property. Kings were first established to defend the republic; they later acquired the power to fight crime and punish injustice. For this reason, they receive a certain income, and they are told what sort of taxes they

---

[6] Ibid., p. XXVI. In his zealous attacks against tyranny, Mariana may appear to espouse anarchy. His major purpose, however, was not to undermine order, but to curb injustice.

[7] Mariana, *Del Rey,* p. 469.

[8] Ibid., p. 479.

[9] Ibid., *Del Rey,* p. 479. [Italics mine.]

may impose. The king has domain over these goods (taxes and royal property), but not over other goods. Furthermore, "if the king is not the owner of private goods, he may not dispose of them (in whole or in part) without the owner's consent". To act otherwise would be tyrannical and coercive and might be cause for excommunication.[10] Mariana's conclusion is that "the king cannot do things which damage the people without their consent (by this I mean to take away their property or part of it)."[11]

Government Expenditures

> How sad it is for the republic and how hateful it is for good people to see those who enter public administration when they are penniless grow rich and fat in public service.[12]

Mariana clearly defined the proper governmental attitude toward fiscal policy. "First of all, after reducing all superfluous spending, the prince must impose moderate taxes." He noted that it is important to balance the budget so that the kingdom will not

> be obliged to go into debt or consume its reserves (the forces of the empire) in payment of interest which will grow daily.[13] . . . Our main concern must be . . . to balance income with expenditures . . . so that the republic is not entangled in more evils because of its inability to pay its debts. If the expenditures of the Crown grow to be larger than taxes, evil will be inevitable. It will be necessary to impose new taxes every day. The citizens will become exasperated and will not listen to the king's mandates.[14]

Domingo de Soto also advised the prince not to exhaust the treasury, urging him not to use the money collected from taxes

[10] Juan de Mariana, *Tratado sobre la Moneda de Vellón,* in *Biblioteca de Autores Españoles,* Rivadeneyra, vol. 31 (Madrid: Editions Atlas, 1950), pp. 578–579.

[11] Ibid., p. 578.

[12] Mariana, *Del Rey,* p. 548.

[13] Ibid.

[14] Ibid.

for expenditures not needed for the common good. "Great dangers for the republic spring from financial exhaustion, the population suffers privations and is greatly oppressed by daily increases in taxes."[15]

Diego de Saavedra Fajardo (1584–1648) recommended that the king maintain a nondeficit budget in which "receipts should be greater than spending."[16] He suggested that the best way to balance the budget is to cut spending[17] because

> power is mad and has to be restrained by economic prudence. Without prudence, empires decline. The Roman Empire declined due to the emperors' excessive spending, which consumed all its treasures.[18]

According to the Late Scholastics, people are much more careless when they spend public money than when they spend their own. This causes expenditures to increase more than they should. In 1619, Pedro Fernandez Navarrete, "Canonist Chaplain and Secretary to his High Majesty", published a book of advice for the preservation of the Spanish monarchy.[19] According to him, Spain's major problem was emigration prompted by the high taxes people had to pay to finance public spending. His conclusion was that the best thing a king could do to enlarge his kingdom was to be moderate in spending. Citing historical precedents, he noted that Nero and Domitian (whom he termed "this world's monsters")

> were obliged to seize possessions from their subjects, deprive soldiers of their pay, leave the army without supplies and the fortress without maintenance and despoil the temples. This was due to *their great*

[15] Domingo de Soto, *De Iustitia et Iure* (Madrid: IEP, 1968), bk. III, qu. VI, art. VII, fol. 98.

[16] Diego de Saavedra Fajardo, *Idea de un Príncipe Político-Cristiano,* in *Biblioteca de Autores Españoles,* vol. 25 (Madrid: Editions Atlas, 1947), p. 191.

[17] Ibid., p. 192.

[18] Ibid., p. 191.

[19] Pedro Fernandez Navarrete, *Conservación de Monarquias* (Madrid: 1619). There is a new edition of this work in *Biblioteca de Autores Españoles,* Rivadeneyra, vol. 25 (Madrid: Editions Atlas, 1947).

*and wasteful spending on nonsensical factories, exquisite banquets, extraor-
dinary clothing, . . . and continuous spectacles and parties.* [20]

Navarrete criticized the enormous number of people living on Spain's
public funds, *"sucking like harpies"* on the king's wealth, while poor
workers could "hardly maintain themselves by eating rye bread and
herbs".[21]

Discarding the notion that abundance of currency denotes wealth,
Navarrete defined a rich province as a *productive* one. He stated that
productivity is hampered when producers have to pay high taxes and
cope with rampant inflation.

> The origin of poverty is high taxes. In continual fear of tax collectors,
> [the farmers] prefer to abandon their land, so they can avoid their
> vexations. As king Teodorico said, the only agreeable country is one
> where no man is afraid of tax collectors.[22]

Furthermore, "he who imposes high taxes receives from very few".[23]
As the number of productive taxpayers declines, "the backs of those
few who are left to bear the burden grow weaker".[24] To lend strength
to his argument, Navarrete mentioned Petrarch who, in a private
letter, advised the king of Sicily that the best policy was to enrich the
subjects and not the treasury.

> The king is not going to be poor if the vassals are rich, because
> riches are better kept in the hands of the subjects than in the
> thrice-locked coffins of the state treasurers, who go bankrupt daily.[25]

Navarrete further declared that those governments that tax production heavily are comparable to the farmworker who harvests the roots
along with the crops. He reinforced his recommendation for tax
reductions with a parable: "If the farmer only takes care of collecting
the fruit and does not cultivate the trees, the orchard is inevitably

---

[20] Ibid., p. 218. [Italics mine.]
[21] Ibid.
[22] Ibid., pp. 105–106.
[23] *"A paucis accipit, qui nimium quarent."* Ibid., p. 130.
[24] Ibid., p. 109.
[25] Ibid.

going to turn into a wasteland in a few years." If, by chance, the king experiences sudden unexpected needs, Navarrete recommended that he solicit voluntary donations. Citing many examples, he declared that the government must not hide its financial problems from its people. "It is not only useless to conceal the maladies when they are public, but it also impedes healing." The will to solve the problem can arise only when there is public knowledge of it.[26]

Navarrete explained that taxes rise when the state increases its expenditures. He then devoted the following twenty-two chapters of his book (Discourses XXIX to L) to an analysis of public spending. Denouncing sixteenth- and seventeenth-century bureaucrats, i.e., the courtiers, he advised that "it is good to dismiss many of them." It is not sufficient to

> prevent future enlargement of the royal court. We need to clean it up and purge it of its present excess of hangers-on. People may say that this is an extreme suggestion since the court supports so many people, but the disease has become so grave and so evident that we have no excuse not to employ the remedy.[27]

Courtiers may become dangerous

> when their excessive spending leads to poverty. Poverty is a bad counselor. It will incite the people to seek in revolution what they lost to waste and vice. Excessive spending leads to high indebtedness and to many controversies.[28]

Another reason to reduce expenditures is that

> since confusion is the mother of all faults, there will inevitably be many delinquents in the intricate jungle of such a court.[29]

Navarrete also criticized those priests who spend more time in the king's palace than in their monastery cells.[30] Since the Spanish court

[26] Ibid., p. 121.
[27] Ibid., p. 171.
[28] Ibid., p. 173.
[29] Ibid., p. 175.
[30] Ibid., p. 177.

was amply supplied with people of low status such as "footmen, coachmen, porters, pastry sellers, waiters and cutthroats", Navarrete prescribed what he called a "copious blood-letting". He declared that even the "good blood" of efficient courtiers must be purged "so that, with it, we can get rid of the bad blood which sustains itself in the shadow of the good".[31]

In *Discurso* XXXI, "On excessive spending", Navarrete quoted Titus' comment that monarchs often lose their kingdoms through excessive governmental expenditures. When people spend a lot,

> they easily fall prey to the temptations of bribery, thievery and other bad actions that violate the laws of justice.
>
> When expenditures exceed the possibilities of the treasury, there is no guarantee of honesty, incorruptible ministers or fair judges.[32]

According to Mariana, whenever it is rumored that the public treasury has been exhausted, the taxpayers become indignant. The frightened prince will then search anxiously for some unusual means of paying his expenses:

> He asks for counsel and receives completely contradictory advice. It is not rare for *the iniquitous and equally useless suggestion of altering the value of money* to be whispered in the king's ear. With this measure, they say, no one will suffer direct harm. The intrinsic value of money will be lower, but the legal value will remain the same. Can you imagine any more easily executed or faster means of extracting the prince from his terrible plight? But how can such learned men come to believe in such a serious mistake and to applaud such a nonsensical plan? A nation, a prince, should never act against justice. Such means, considered from every perspective, are and always will be plunder (*latrocinium*). How can it be otherwise if I am obliged to pay five for what is worth three? If money has come to be a general medium of exchange, it is precisely because of its stability of value, subject to only a few oscillations in times of great crisis.[33]

---

[31] Ibid., p. 179.

[32] Ibid., p. 209.

[33] Juan de Mariana, *Biblioteca de Autores Españoles,* vol. 30, Discurso Preliminar, p. XXXVI. [Italics mine.]

The last chapter of Mariana's book on inflation deals with the ultimate cause of currency debasement, i.e., excessive public spending. Although he denied being a specialist on this topic, he sounds like one. Royal expenditures, he declared, should be reduced. "Moderate spending, if it is done with order, shines more and shows more majesty than disorderly superflous spending." He then explained that in 1429, royal expenditures totaled approximately *"8 cuentos de maravedis"*.[34]

> Some people will say that this account is very old, that things have changed a lot, that kings are very powerful, and for this reason they need to spend more and their maintenance is more expensive. This is true, but it cannot explain the disproportionate spending that takes place today in the royal house.[35]

Noting that by 1564 expenditures had reached 118 "cuentos of maravedis", he remarked,

> You will say then: which expenditures can be reduced? I do not understand the subject; those who are working in this field must know. What I know is that people are saying that spending is being undertaken without order and that there are no books or reasons to explain how income is spent.[36]

Mariana then advised the king to reduce the granting of subsidies. He enjoined the monarch not to spend the assets the kingdom grants him with the kind of freedom enjoyed by the private owner of a vineyard. Spain, he wrote, was overwhelmed with "public prizes, *encomiendas,* pensions, benefits and offices". Lest the prince believe that granting privileges will buy him friends, Mariana warned that "Men are more often motivated by hope than by gratitude."[37] Furthermore, he advised the king to stop engaging in what he termed unnecessary wars and nonessential enterprises. As did Navarrete, Mariana recommended the amputation of "cancerous extremities" that cannot be healed:

---

[34] *"Cuento"* means one million. One mark of silver (eight ounces) was coined into sixty-seven *reales* (silver pieces); and one *real* was worth thirty-four *maravedis.*

[35] Mariana, *Tratado,* p. 591.

[36] Ibid.

[37] Ibid.

It is said that in the last few years there is not a single job or dignity—including audiences and bishoprics—that was not bought with gifts and bribes.... This should not be true.... It is terrible that people are saying it.... We see ministers, recently risen from the dust of the earth, suddenly loaded with a thousand ducats in rent. *Where is this money coming from if it is not from the blood of the poor and the flesh of businessmen?*[38]

He cited the historical case of a Jewish advisor to the monarch of Castille who informed the civil servants that he knew they were pilfering public funds. By promising that they would be forgiven if they gave the king half of their ill-gotten gains, he was able to recover vast sums.[39] Mariana counseled that the king should exercise strict control over the activities of public servants. He suggested that they submit an inventory of the goods they own at the moment they take office, so that afterward they can be obliged to explain in detail how they got the rest.[40]

In response to the idea that "the common good" justifies increased government spending, Bartolome de Albornóz noted that in a republic, government should respect private property.

It is a general rule that the public good must be placed before the private good, but it is difficult to know what the public good is.... Many times, Satan transforms himself into the Angel of Light, and we treat what is unreasonable as good.... I ask the reader to read [in Portugese history] about the extremely sumptuous palace constructed by a pagan king. On its grounds was the hut of an old lady who had refused to sell it to the king. He showed this building to everyone so they could see how just a king he was and how much freedom his subjects enjoyed.[41]

[38] Ibid. [Italics mine.]
[39] Ibid.
[40] Ibid.
[41] Bartolomé de Albornóz, *Arte de los Contratos* (Valencia, 1573), p. 69.

Principles of Taxation

> Taxes are commonly a calamity for the people and a nightmare for
> the government. For the former they are always excessive; for the
> latter they are never enough, never too much.[42]

The Doctors defined taxes as that which the prince or the republic
takes from private people to sustain the community, i.e., a legal
transfer of property from the individual to the government. They
acknowledged that both the king and the people are capable of
injustices in this regard. According to Pedro de Navarra,

> Taxes can be tyrannical, not only if the one who imposes them does
> not have the legal faculty, but also if one is taxed more heavily than
> others or if tax funds are used for a particular good or for the
> prince's interest instead of for public utility. In cases of extreme
> necessity, laymen are not, in conscience, obliged to pay.[43]

Stating that within the limits of legal justice, people may do what
they like with their property, the Late Scholastics posited three
exceptions. Although they have full right of domain, young persons
enjoy only a limited right to use their property. The court may also
limit the use of a thief's property or rule that some of his goods be
transferred to another as restitution. Third, the government can appropriate goods in the form of taxes.[44]

Nonetheless, not every tax law is just, and it is not always unjust to
evade taxes. Just tax legislation must first fulfill the requirements for

[42] Mariana, *Biblioteca de Autores Españoles,* Discurso Preliminar, p. XXXVI.
[43] Pedro de Navarra, *De Restitutione* (Toledo, 1597), p. 124.
[44] See p. 61, above.

any just law.[45] In addition, it must meet another set of requirements concerning need (is there a legitimate necessity for new tax laws?), opportunity (is it the right moment to impose such taxes?), form (are the proposed taxes proportionate and equitable?) and level (are the proposed taxes moderate or excessive?). Navarra wrote that the use of taxes to support the prince's interests constitutes tyrannical confiscation and plunder.[46] He further stated that if the cause for which a tax has been established ceases to exist, by natural law the citizens are not obliged to pay.[47] Villalobos declared that the king's advisers

> must realize that taxes severely weaken towns and impoverish farmers. We can see places which yesterday were flourishing and had many inhabitants and now lie prostrated and fallow because farmers cannot tolerate high taxes.[48]

In the light of their own political circumstances, the Late Scholastics analyzed the burden of taxation with great courage. Modern thinkers may say with Navarrete and king Teodorico that "the only agreeable country is the one where no one is afraid of tax collectors."[49]

[45] In Thomist doctrine, that which is not just does not constitute a true law. St. Thomas Aquinas, *Summa Theologica* (London: Blackfriars, 1975), I–II, qu. 95, art. 2. This argument refers back to St. Augustine's dictum "that which is not just seems to be no law at all". (*De Lib. Arb.* i. 5). To be just, a law must derive from the law of nature in accordance with the rules of reason and usefulness to man. The just law must also be possible in the context of the customs of the country. It must be formulated by the one who governs the community, but it may not exceed his power as a lawgiver. The subjects should bear the burden of the law in accordance with proportional equality. St. Thomas declared that unjust laws impose burdens "inequally on the community, although with a view to the common good". He further decreed that "the like are acts of violence rather than laws". I–II, Q. 96, art. 4.

[46] Navarra, *De Restitutione,* p. 135.

[47] Ibid., p. 137.

[48] Henrique de Villalobos, *Summa de la Theologia Moral y Canónica* (Barcelona, 1632), p. 91.

[49] Ibid., pp. 105–106. [Italics mine.]

5

THE THEORY OF MONEY

The Schoolmen developed their theory of money in accordance with
Aristotelian teachings. They believed that the inconveniences of barter gave rise to the need for money. The essential function of money is
to serve as a medium of exchange. St. Thomas Aquinas reminded his
readers that

> money, . . . according to Aristotle, was invented chiefly for exchanges
> to be made, so that the prime and proper use of money is its use and
> disbursement in the way of ordinary transactions.[1]

Money could also be used as a store of value and as a measure for
exchanges. These two functions, however, depended on the essence
of money (i.e., money as the most commonly used medium of
exchange).

Soto explained the nature and origin of money in Aristotelian
terms and observed that "the construction of a house cannot be
estimated in terms of shoes, socks or other manufactured goods".
Calculation is impossible without money (a unit of measurement).[2]
Although he said that money could be made of many different
materials, Soto preferred gold coins.[3]

---

[1] St. Thomas Aquinas, *Summa Theologica* (London: Blackfriars, 1975), II–II, qu.
78, art. 5, resp. The Latin text reads: *"Pecunia autem, secundum Philosophum, principaliter
est inventa ad commutationes faciendas."*

[2] Domingo de Soto, *De Iustitia et Iure* (Madrid: IEP, 1968), bk. III, qu. V, art 4,
fol. 88.

[3] Ibid.

Money and Prices

The Medieval Schoolmen also studied the effect that an increase in the money supply (or a process of currency debasement) has on prices. This portion of their analysis is of great interest to many modern authors.[4] Mariana pointed out that "if the legal value of the currency is reduced, the prices of all goods will, without fail, increase in the same proportion".[5] He noted that currency debasement will produce the same results.[6]

In his *Manual de Confesores y Penitentes* (Manual for Confessors and Penitents), the theologian Martín de Azpilcueta provided what many authors consider to be the first formulation of the quantity theory of money:

> other things being equal, in countries where there is a great scarcity of money, all other saleable goods, and even the hands and labour of men, are given for less money than where it is abundant. Thus we see by experience that in France, where money is scarcer than in Spain, bread, wine, cloth and labour are worth much less. And even in Spain, in times when money is scarcer, saleable goods and labour were given for very much less than after the discovery of the Indies, which flooded the country with gold and silver. The reason for this is that money is worth more where and when it is scarce than where and when it is abundant. What some men say, that a scarcity of money brings down other things, arises from the fact that its excessive rise [in value] makes other things seem lower, just as a short man

---

[4] *The School of Salamanca: Readings in Spanish Monetary Theory, 1544–1605* (Oxford: Clarendon Press, 1952) by Marjorie Grice-Hutchinson devotes special attention to this topic.

[5] Juan de Mariana, *Tratado sobre la Moneda de Vellón*, in *Biblioteca de Autores Españoles* Rivadeneyra vol. 31 (Madrid: Editions Atlas, 1950): p. 586. Mariana added, that "What we are saying here is not a fantasy of our dreams, since every time this was done the same result followed." Ibid.

[6] Ibid.

standing beside a very tall one looks shorter than when he is beside a man of his own height.[7]

Albornóz also deduced that an abundance of currency was the cause of high prices in Spain. Everything was expensive except money. He emphasized that "this is the most essential and subtle principle regarding this matter".[8]

Nearly all the Late Scholastics shared the idea that the quantity of money is one of the main factors influencing its value. Luis de Molina explained

> There is another way in which money may be worth more in one place than in another; namely, because it is scarcer there than elsewhere. Other things being equal, wherever money is most abundant, there it will be least valuable for the purpose of buying goods and comparing things other than money. Just as an abundance of goods causes prices to fall (the quantity of money and number of merchants being equal), so does an abundance of money cause them to rise (the quantity of goods and number of merchants being equal). The reason is that the money itself becomes less valuable for the purpose of buying and comparing goods. Thus we see that in Spain the purchasing power of money is far lower, on account of its abundance, than it was eighty years ago. A thing that could be bought for two ducats at that time is nowadays worth 5, 6 or even more. Wages have risen in the same proportion, and so have dowries, the price of estates, the income from benefices and other things.
>
> We likewise see that money is far less valuable in the New World (especially in Peru, where it is more plentiful) than it is in Spain. But in places where it is scarcer than in Spain, it will be more valuable. Nor will the value of money be the same in all other places, but will vary; and this will be due to variations in its quantity, other things being equal. . . . Even in Spain itself, the value of money varies: it is usually lowest of all in Seville, where the ships come in from the New World and where for that reason money is most abundant.

[7] Martín de Azpilcueta, *Manual de Confesores y Penitentes* (Coimbra, 1553), p. 84, English translation in Grice-Hutchinson, *The School of Salamanca* (Oxford: Clarendon Press, 1952), pp. 80–96 and in Grice-Hutchinson *Early Economic Thought in Spain, 1177–1740* (London: Allen & Unwin, 1975), p. 104.

[8] Bartolome de Albornóz, *Arte de la Contratos* (Valencia, 1573), p. 132.

Wherever the demand for money is greatest, whether for buying or carrying goods, . . . or for any other reason, there its value will be highest. It is these things, too, that cause the value of money to vary in the course of time in one and the same place.[9]

People's ideas concerning money also influence its exchange value. Utility alone is not the source of value. Rather, utility and scarcity together determine it. Molina specified that in the exchange of goods (barter) and in the exchange of money what matters is not their intrinsic value, but "the extrinsic value, that is accidental and depends on esteem".[10] In money, as in

venal things the price does not follow the nature of them, and they are not priced according to their innate dignity but according to the need we have for them and their usefulness.[11]

Molina then explained that "in money exchanges we must take into account not the value that is in its nature but the estimation of that value".[12]

Mariana delineated two factors that lower the value of money:

The first is the plentifulness of this money, which causes a reduction in its value and increases the quantities of goods that must be traded for it. The second is that this money is so debased and of such poor quality that everyone will try to avoid having it in their homes. People will not be willing to sell their commodities except for large sums of this money.[13]

A currency that undergoes constant debasement loses its usefulness. People then tend to reduce their cash holdings, which further undermines the value of money.

---

[9] Luis de Molina, *De Iustitia et Iure* (Moguntiae, 1614), disp. 406, cols. 704–705.
[10] Ibid.
[11] Ibid.
[12] Ibid.
[13] "*La una ser, como será, mucha sin número y sin cuenta, que hace abaratar cualquiera cosa que sea, y por el contrario, encarecer lo que por ella se trueca; la segunda ser moneda tan baja y tan mala, que todos la querrán echar de su casa y los que tienen las mercaderías no las querrán dar sino por mayor cuantía.*" Mariana, *Tratado*, p. 587.

Two things were certain for Mariana: first, that the king has the power to change the money (power to change the seal and shape of the coins); and second, that in case of great necessities, for instance, the king can debase the money provided that (a) it is for a short period of time and (b) once the crisis has ended, the king will make restitution for the damage caused to the people. It is obvious that Mariana saw currency debasement as a form of taxation.[14]

Fray Tomás de Mercado also assigned considerable importance to the influence the estimation of money exercises on prices:

> The third reason that is regarded as the foundation of the exchanges is the diversity that exists in the estimation. And in order to understand it (for it is a very weighty reason) we must realize that the value and price of money are not the same thing as its estimation. A clear proof of this is that in the Indies money is worth the same as here; that is to say, a *real* is worth 34 *maravedis*. A *peso* is worth 13 *reales*, and its price is the same in Spain, but although the value and price are the same, the estimation is very different in both places. For money is esteemed much less in the Indies than in Spain. The quality and disposition of the country engender in the hearts of all who enter it so generous a temper that they esteem a dozen *reales* of no greater value than a dozen *maravedis* here.[15]

The same author wrote that

> in money we can find two things: one is its value and its legal standard that are the substance and nature of money; the other is the esteem. In the way that what in other things is extrinsic and variable, in money is natural and essential, and the estimation is accidental.[16]

In 1553, Domingo de Soto applied these doctrines to contemporary conditions in Spain, observing that

> The more plentiful money is in Medina, the more unfavorable are the terms of exchange, and the higher the price that must be paid by

[14] Ibid.

[15] Tomás de Mercado, *Suma de Tratos y Contratos* (Salamanca, 1594), pp. 92–93, quoted in Grice-Hutchinson, *Early Economic Thought,* p. 105.

[16] Ibid.

whoever wishes to send money from Spain to Flanders, since the demand for money is less in Spain than in Flanders. And the scarcer money is in Medina, the less he need pay there, because more people want money in Medina than are sending it to Flanders.[17]

Soto believed that the value of money could be changed in times of great crisis, but very rarely was it legal to do so. "On the contrary, money should imitate natural law, always firm and fixed."[18] The prince who enacts successive variations in the value of money usually loses the trust of his subjects.

Cardinal Juan de Lugo shared similar views:

It is to be noted with Lessius, Molina and Salas that the excess of this unequal value that money has in different places is not derived only from the higher intrinsic value of money, proceeding from its superior metal content or higher legal tale, but may also be caused by the diversity in its extrinsic value. Thus, in the place to which the money is sent, there may be a general scarcity of money or more people may require it or there may be better opportunities for doing business with it and making a profit. And, since money will there be more useful for satisfying human needs, more goods will be bought than elsewhere with the same sum of money, therefore money will rightly be regarded as more valuable in that place.[19]

Covarrubias also declared that the estimation of money will vary with the purity of the metal content of the coin.[20] Taking things further, Juan de Medina indicated that although the legal value of money should be invariable, the quality of the coin will vary. The money that has more value is the one that is longer lasting and easier to carry.[21]

---

[17] Soto, *De Iustitia,* bk. 7, qu. 5, art. 2. Translation from Grice-Hutchinson, *Early Economic Thought,* p. 103.

[18] Ibid., bk. III, qu. 5, art. 4, fol. 88.

[19] Juan de Lugo, *De Iustitia et Iure* (Lyon: 1642), dis. 26, sec. 4, paras. 41–44, quoted in Grice-Hutchinson, *Early Economic Thought,* p. 106.

[20] Diego Covarrubias y Leiva, *Opera Omnia* (Salamanca, 1577), bk. 1, chap. 7, p. 1055.

[21] "Facilius potest de loco in locum portasi." Juan de Medina, *De Contractibus* (Salamanca, 1550), p. 148.

Medina cited other factors influencing the value of money: (1) its capacity to serve as a store of value,[22] (2) the number of places accepting that kind of money,[23] (3) The variability of its legal value[24] (i.e., the higher the variability, the lower the value of money). Medina concluded that the actual value of money differs from the legal value imposed by authority. This difference in value is founded not only on reasons of the objective quality of the coin, but also on the *utility* of the type of money involved.[25]

Other authors, quoted less by historians, wrote in similar terms. Pedro de Navarra said, "Among free people, if a coin is devalued in weight and quality, its value and estimation are also going to be reduced, either when one accepts it in an exchange or when one uses it for a purchase."[26] For Cristobal de Villalón, the value of money changes every day "because it is valued daily according to the market".[27] Many eighteenth-century authors shared these concepts. Dominguez, for example, explained that money had an intrinsic and an extrinsic value and then concluded that while the former is founded on the legal standard determined by the authorities, the latter is variable and depends on the market price of the metal content of the coin.

---

[22] Gold was in this sense the best money since *"quia melius domi conservatur aurea quam alier moneter."* Ibid.

[23] *"Quia una universalius est distrahibilis, quia in pluribus regnis & locis currit & expenditur quam alia."* Ibid.

[24] *"Quia not ita facile valor legalis bonae pecunie variatur, sicut valor aliarum pecuniarum inferiorum, quae magis sunt periculo diminutionis exponiter."* Ibid.

[25] The Latin quotation reads: *"Itaque non solum aurea pecunia valet plus quam alia inferior moneta: ratione materiae, sed etiam quatenus pecunia est, & talis qualitatis dicitur plus valere ob praefatas & alias* utilitates, *in quibus una moneta aliis monetiis est preferenda: ideo dicunt hac ratione posse pecuniam vendi carius, quam sit valor eius legalis."* Ibid.

[26] Pedro de Navarra, *De Restitutione* (Toledo, 1597), bk. II, p. 177. The Latin text reads: *"Sed illi liberi sunt, ut si moneta diminuta sit in materia, & pondere, ipsi etiam de valore et aestimatione diminuant, eam sic recipendo, et expendendum."*

[27] Cristobal de Villalón, *Provechoso Tratado de Cambios y Contrataciones de Mercaderes y Reprovación de Usura* (Valladolid, 1542), fol XI. (The Spanish text reads: *"conforme a la plaza"* [according to the market]).

The value of money, undoubtedly, is like the value of everything under the sun: it is determined in accordance with the price which they [the people] are willing to assign.[28]

Dominguez ridiculed those authors who espoused a different price theory for money than for other goods. Were we to adopt such a system, he remarked, "we should need a special name for each contract", and this would be absurd.[29]

Currency Debasement and Private Property

Many Late Scholastics disapproved of currency debasement as a means of redistributing wealth. While the king might derive short-term benefits from such a policy, a sound, stable currency was far more important. Mercado noted that

among the things necessary for good government and peace in the kingdom, one is that the value and tale of the money, and even its seal and design, must be durable and as invariable as possible.[30]

He also criticized changes in money because they affect

the wealth of every person. In the end everything is money, and so everything is changed; the poor become rich and the rich poor. It is for this reason that Aristotle says that among the stable and durable things that a republic ought to have is a currency valued at the same price, if possible, for twenty generations, and the great-grandsons will know what they inherited from their great-grandparents and

---

[28] J. M. Dominguez, *Discursos Jurídicos* (Madrid, 1732), p. 65. The complete title of this book is *Discursos Jurídicos sobre las Aceptaciones, Pagas, Interesses, y demás Requisitos, y Qualidades, de las Letras de Cambio.* The author was born in Seville, the book is dedicated to the Archbishop of Valencia and has the approval of the Inquisition (as no part of the text is in opposition to the Holy Catholic Faith and good customs; in Spanish it reads *"por no contener cosa que se oponga a nuestra Santa Fe Catholica y buenas costumbres".*)

[29] Ibid.

[30] Mercado, *Suma de Tratos,* p. 264.

what in their goodness they increased, gained and left to their children.[31]

Juan de Mariana compared the transfer of wealth through currency debasement to the action of someone who goes into private barns and steals a portion of the crops stored there:

> the king has no domain over the goods of the people, and he can not take them in whole or in part. We can see then: would it be licit for the king to go into a private barn taking for himself half of the wheat and trying to satisfy the owner by saying that he can sell the rest at twice the price? I do not think we can find a person with such depraved judgment as to approve this, yet the same is done with copper coins.[32]

Mariana noted that when the king coined new money, he kept two-thirds of its value while allowing his subjects the other third.[33] Predicting that "the people will become altered and impoverished", Mariana applied the term "infamous systematic robbery"[34] to such manipulation of the money supply.

Inconveniences Caused by Currency Debasement

Mariana ascribed great importance to sound money. Money, together with weights and measures, is the basis of commerce and contracts. For that reason he said that,

> as the foundations of a building must be firm and stable, weights, measures and money should not be changed if one wants to avoid the confusion and the pendulum swings of commerce.[35]

---

[31] Ibid., pp. 265–266.
[32] Mariana, *Tratado*, p. 586.
[33] Ibid., p. 587.
[34] *"Infame latrocinio."* Ibid.
[35] Ibid.

Quoting Leviticus 27:23, Mariana stipulated that the "purity and just price" of money should be guarded in the temple.[36] The shekel stored in the temple should be the standard of value. He also quoted St. Thomas Aquinas and advised the prince not to alter the currency at his will.[37] Modifications in money

> cause great confusion when one wants to adjust the old to the new and one nation to another. It seems that those who are in government are not very learned persons because they have not noticed the tribulations and revolts that occurred for this reason in other nations and in our own backyard. Nor have they learned how careful one must be when dealing with these matters. It is easy to understand that this arbitrary means of debasing the money can be advantageous in the short run for the prince and that it has been used many times. But at the same time we have to realize the negative effects which have always followed and how it has always caused great damage to the people and even to the prince, obliging him to retrace his steps and try to solve the problem with even worse means, as we shall see below.[38]

Attempting to solve economic problems by debasing the currency, according to Mariana, was like giving a sick person an alcoholic beverage. First it refreshes him, but later it causes accidents and worsens the malady.[39] Mariana explained that the king could use poor-quality coins to pay his debts and alleviate some of his problems. He also added that, in the short run, the increase in the money supply could cause an increase in production. People would then increase their demand for goods as "everyone will try to get rid of this debased money".[40] Noting that the majority of currency-debasing tyrants

[36] *"Omnis aestimatis siclo sanctuari ponderatur."* Ibid.

[37] St. Thomas Aquinas, *De Regim. Princ.,* lib. 11, cap. 14. English ed. *On Kingship to the King of Cyprus* (the Governance of Rulers), trans. I.T. Eschmann (Toronto: The Pontifical Institute of Mediaeval Studies, 1949).

[38] Mariana, *Tratado,* p. 587. The "worse means" were price controls. Mariana stipulated that it would be a mistake to impose them. Stating that "no one will want to sell his goods", he remarked that such a "remedy" would not cure, but worsen the situation. Ibid., p. 586.

[39] Ibid., p. 581.

[40] Ibid.

adopted copper money (*vellon* money) with no silver or gold content at all,[41] Mariana formulated what later came to be called "Gresham's Law". When copper money is abundant and overvalued, it drives out silver coinage (which is artificially undervalued).[42]

In the tenth chapter of his treatise on money, Mariana listed the grave inconveniences that follow a process of artificial increase in the money supply. He began by proving that this action violates the law of Spain. According to him, it is acceptable to use copper money only for commercial dealings of small value. Money was "invented to ease and help commerce", which is its main function. The best money is that which performs its function best. It is not necessary to have silver and gold money alone or to forbid the use of copper coins, he said, but "we don't have to go to the other extreme and be innundated with copper money".[43]

Furthermore, Mariana averred that currency debasement contradicts both reason and natural law. Since it violates property rights, it is equivalent to plunder. In this light, it is also unjust to offer debased currency in payment of debts incurred in sound money.[44] Mariana noted that this is not done with other goods because the king does not own them. He implied that whenever the king has the power to administer goods, it is reasonable to expect fraud.

For Mariana, one of the most negative effects of currency debasement occurs in the political arena. The king will suffer if his income decreases. Commercial activities will diminish, and the poverty of the people will lead to the poverty of the kingdom.[45] People will grow to hate the prince.[46] Despite the verity of these affirmations, Mariana noted that

> Covetousness blinds, need causes distress, and the past is forgotten; in this way we repeat mistakes very easily. I confess the truth: I

[41] Ibid.
[42] "Everyone prefers to pay with copper money rather than with silver money." Ibid, p. 587.
[43] Ibid., p. 586.
[44] Ibid.
[45] Ibid. p. 587.
[46] Ibid., p. 588.

marvel that those who work in government have not learned from these examples.[47]

He defined currency debasement as a sort of tax and commented that such taxation is "very difficult to bear in this sad kingdom full of tribulations".[48] In the light of these abundant arguments, he concluded,

> I understand that any alteration of money is dangerous. It can never be good to debase currency or to fix its price higher than its natural valuation and common estimation.[49]

Some lines later Mariana advised that it would be better to leave things as they are, without modifying the money, because the only one who can profit from currency debasement is the prince, "and we should not always look after the prince's interests, and least of all when he uses these methods".[50]

Saavedra Fajardo also recommended that the prince refrain from altering the value of money. Coins are like young girls, he said. It is an offense to touch them. Money problems create contract problems and since commerce is hindered by these changes, the republic also suffers.[51] Upon assuming power, all kings should promise that they will not alter the money. They should see to it that money is maintained in substance, form and quantity. Saavedra Fajardo defined sound money as currency that has a value equivalent to the price of its metal content plus the minting cost. Local coins should be similar in purity to the ones more widely used, and foreign coins should be allowed to circulate in the kingdom.[52]

Mariana decried monetary debasement, calling it a "barbaric" practice. Those who propose such a thing, he wrote, can justly be described as a "plague in the republic".[53]

---

[47] Ibid.

[48] Ibid., p. 589.

[49] Ibid., p. 591.

[50] Ibid.

[51] Diego de Saavedra Fajardo, *Idea de un Príncipe Pólitico-Cristiano,* in *Biblioteca de Autores Españoles,* Rivadeneyra, vol. 25 (Madrid: Editions Atlas, 1947), p. 192.

[52] Ibid., p. 193.

[53] Mariana, *Biblioteca de Autores Españoles,* introduction to vol. 30, p. XXXVI.

If we take the liberty of reducing the fineness of gold and silver coins by two percent or more . . . foreign commerce will become impossible if local merchants don't acquiesce to suffering a loss equivalent to the devaluation. Distrust will characterize domestic commerce, and a paralysis of production will necessarily follow, producing scarcity, high prices, poverty, confusion, disorder. It is true that government can oblige me to accept the new money for my goods but, could I not, at the same time, increase the price of the goods until I am compensated for the loss the arbitrary adulteration of metals inflicts on me? Would not all the efforts of the king to surmount this development, which stems from the natural desire of all people to protect their own interests, be completely useless? *Such sad results flow so spontaneously from the condition of the human character that to forsee them we have only to consult our reason. But it is not only reason that teaches us this, it is experience, a truly macabre experience, which writes its message in blood and tears.*[54]

[54] Ibid. [Italics mine.]

6

COMMERCE, MERCHANTS AND TRADESMEN

The moralist's attitude toward commerce is of extreme importance for the development of a market economy. By the time of the Schoolmen, commerce had long been held in low esteem by moralists of different countries, ages and backgrounds. Although most of the Late Scholastics found commercial activities to be morally indifferent, they outlined the advantages of commerce, turning their attention first to the critical arguments of the Church fathers and the Canonists. St. Thomas Aquinas' justification of mercantile profits offered many examples of the benefits that commerce may bring to a society. He regarded three commercial activities as explicitly useful for society: (a) the conservation and storing of goods, (b) the importation of useful goods that are necessary for the republic, (c) the transportation of goods from places where they are abundant to places where they are scarce.[1]

As is proper in Scholastic tradition, Domingo de Soto studied both sides of the issue. He first presented the negative arguments: "Barter is simpler than commerce, direct exchange is simpler than indirect exchange, and it causes fewer problems. For many centuries humanity was happier living without money." Proceeding to point out the benefits of commerce, Soto then defined contracts as obligations and acknowledged that both parties profit from the arrangement.[2] Furthermore, he confirmed that "buying and selling are very necessary contracts for the republic". Basing his arguments on Aristotelian

---

[1] St. Thomas Aquinas, *Summa Theologica* (London: Blackfriars, 1975), II–II, qu. 77, art. 4.

[2] "I give you this amount of goods and you give me this amount of money, and this is not an identity." Domingo de Soto, *De Iustitia et Iure* (Madrid: IEP, 1968), bk. VI, qu. II, art. 1, fol. 193.

reasonings, Soto explained that it was natural for direct exchange to be gradually replaced by indirect exchange:

> Mankind progresses from imperfection to perfection. For this reason, in the beginning barter was sufficient as man was rude and ignorant and had few necessities. But afterward, with the development of a more educated, civilized and distinguished life, the need to create new forms of trade arose. Among them the most respectable is commerce, despite the fact that human avarice can pervert anything.[3]

Conceding St. Augustine's point that business "is like eating, a morally indifferent act, which can be good or bad depending the ends and the circumstances".[4] Soto reiterated his conclusion that

> commerce is necessary for the republic. Not all the provinces have the goods they need in abundance. On the contrary, due to climates some have in abundance the fruits and labors which are scarce in others and vice versa.[5]

Soto emphasized that to survive, the republic needs to have people who transport goods from the places where they are abundant to the places where they are scarce.[6]

As to whether it would not be "more prudent" to charge public servants with this responsibility, Soto held that such restricted trade would not suffice for the wide spectrum of necessary goods.[7] Carrying this point further, Mariana suggested that commerce favors the common good. God gave man his nature of social dependency and his limited ability and capacity so that man would feel the need for commerce.

---

[3] Ibid.

[4] Ibid., art. 2, fol. 194.

[5] Ibid.

[6] "And what we say of different places [provinces] can be said also of different times. A people can enjoy an abundance of goods in certain times and great scarcity in others. Without people to respond appropriately to such circumstances the republic could not do without harm." Ibid.

[7] Ibid.

He thus prefers to live in society and to enjoy the benefits of social cooperation (i.e., division of labor).[8]

International Trade

The Doctors dealt with international trade in a discussion similar to their remarks concerning domestic trade. The few differences in their public-policy recommendations regarding international trade relate to their advice concerning taxes.[9] One of the principal contributions of the Late Scholastics regarding commerce consists of the recognition of international free trade as subject to human laws, as Vitoria established in his *De Indis et de Iure Belli Relectiones.*[10] Vitoria's point of view led Teofilo Urdanoz to state "that no one has realized, at least up to now,

---

[8] "For God, the Parent and Creator of the human race, saw that nothing would be more valuable to man than mutual charity and friendship, and that it would not be possible for mutual affection to be cherished and fostered among men unless they were gathered into a body in one place and subject to the same law. . . . He created men to desire this and move toward it with true necessity, lacking many things and subject to many dangers and evils. . . . Thus He, who gave food and covering to the other animals and armed them against external force by giving some of them horns or teeth or claws, and others swift feet to fly from danger, cast as if he had lost his all in a shipwreck. . . . The rest of life is like its beginning, and proves to lack many things which neither an individual nor a small group could obtain for themselves. How much work and industry is involved in combing, spinning and weaving linen, wool and silk. . . . The life of no single man is long enough to obtain all these things, however long he lives, unless the wonder and observation of many men, and collective experience, should come to the rescue." Juan de Mariana, *Del Rey y de la Institución Real,* chap. i, quoted in Bernice Hamilton, *Political Thought in Sixteenth-Century Spain* (Oxford: Clarendon Press, 1963), p. 32.

[9] Import and export duties do not appear to have been very high (12.5 percent). Leonardo Lessio, *De Iustitia et dure* (Antwerp, 1626), lib. 2, cap. 32, p. 404. Most of the Medieval Schoolmen proposed placing a higher tax on imported luxury goods than on other goods. The reasons they proffered were prompted mainly by fiscal and distributive motives (taxes on food imports, for example, would greatly reduce the standard of living of poor workmen).

[10] Francisco de Vitoria, *De Indis et de Iure Belli Relectiones,* Ed. Ernest Nys (New York: Oceana, 1964), p. 153.

that Vitoria's vision of the right to free communication and unrestricted foreign relations represents an *explicit advance of the principles of economic neoliberalism and worldwide free market.* "[11] Describing the advantages of commerce between the Indians and the Spaniards, Vitoria claimed that "the native princes cannot prevent their subjects from trading with the Spaniards". He said the same of the Spanish prince. Eternal, natural and positive human law (*ius gentium*) favors international trade. To abjure it would violate the Golden Rule. Vitoria denominated the laws restricting foreign trade, with the objective of excluding a foreign country from sharing in the benefit "iniquitous and against charity". Quoting Ovid, he added that "man is not a wolf for other men", and that "nature has established a certain bond between men".[12] International trade should respect the prices that prevail in each region according to common estimation. Wide differences in appreciation do not render the exchange unjust. Molina reasoned that

> it does not seem proper to condemn those exchanges based on the common estimation of the goods in a specific region, even if this could at times cause laughter due to the primitive nature and customs of those who take part in the exchange. We have already discussed this subject when we spoke about slavery. To summarize, the just price of goods depends principally on the common estimation of the men of each region. When a good is sold in a certain region or place at a certain price (without fraud or monopoly or any foul play), that price should be held as a rule and measure to judge the just price of said good in that region or place, as long as the circumstances which might cause the price to increase or decrease remain stable.[13]

[11] Father Teofilo Urdanoz, *Sintesis teológico-juridica de las Doctrinas de Vitoria,* in Francisco de Vitoria, *Relectio de Indis o Libertad de los Indios, Corpus Hispanorum de Pace,* vol. V, critical edition by L. Perena and J. M. Perez Prendes, introductory studies by V. Beltrán de Heredia, R. Agostino Iannarone, T. Urdanoz and A. Truyol y L. Perena (Madrid: Consejo Superior de Investigaciones Científicas, 1967), p. CXL.

[12] Francisco de Vitoria, *Relecciones sobre los Indios,* in Restituto Sierra Bravo, *El Pensamiento Social y Económico de la Escolástica* (Madrid: Consejo Superior de Investigaciones Cientificas, 1975), vol. 2, p. 622, and in *De Indis et de iure belli relectiones* Ed. Ernest Nys, (New York: Oceana, 1964), p. 153.

[13] Luis de Molina, *De Iustitia et Iure* (Madrid: Ed. Nacional, 1981) p. 169.

Cristobal de Villalón recognized that international trade would reduce production costs and benefit those who engaged in it. It thus serves the common good. "In the same way that in order to live more happily and with greater ease, a province which lacks a certain product should buy it where this good is abundant. This allows people to achieve possession of the goods with less cost and work and to enjoy them with happiness and pleasure."[14]

Juan de Mariana indicated that it was "convenient to protect international trade with moderate taxes". Believing that the "object and nature of commerce" is to facilitate the easy exchange of needed goods, he noted that "the higher the price of the goods, the smaller the number of buyers". Mariana therefore recommended implementing policies to preserve low prices on imported goods.[15]

The exchange of goods with foreign merchants is, for Bartolome de Albornóz, the "most natural [contract] that exists in humanity". Furthermore, he stated that

> it is more immutable, and less subject to variations and alterations than other parts of civil law. . . . Buying and selling is the nerve of human life that sustains the universe. By means of buying and selling the world is united, joining distant lands and nations, people of different languages, laws and ways of life. If it were not for these contracts, some would lack the goods that others have in abundance, and they would not be able to share the goods that they have in excess with those countries where they are scarce.[16]

Albornóz cited many examples of international trade between the barbaric nations, the East and West Indies and others, concluding that there were differences in the modes of production, not only between countries, but also within the provinces of Spain. He agreed with St. Bernardino of Siena that what in one land is abundant and of low

---

[14] Cristobal de Villalón, *Provechoso Tratado de Cambios y Contrataciones de Mercaderes y Reprobación de Usura* (Valladolid: Francisco Fernandez de Cordoba, 1542), fol. X.

[15] Mariana, *Del Rey,* p. 550.

[16] Bartolome de Albornóz, *Arte de los Contratos* (Valencia, 1573), chap. 7, p. 29.

price may be necessary, uncommon and expensive in another.[17] St. Bernardino entrusted responsibility to the tradesmen who "take the goods to be sold in those places where they are scarce, sometimes receiving in return [as a price] the goods they [the countries] have in abundance".[18]

With this sort of reasoning, it is not surprising that some years later, Lessio surmised that

> if, without cause, the magistrates exclude foreign sellers, and for that reason the price of the good in question is increased, they have to compensate the citizens for the damage caused by that increase.[19]

---

[17] St. Bernardino of Siena, *Opera Omnia* (Venice, 1591), p. 311. The text in Latin reads: *"Quia quod in una terra est abundans & vile, hoc idem in alia terra est necessarium, rarum & carum."*

[18] Ibid., p. 62.

[19] *"Sicut si Magistratus sine causa excluderet alios venditores, & ita mercium tuarum pretium valde excresceret teneretur ille civibus compensare damnum illius incrementi."* Lessio, *De Iustitia*, p. 280.

7

VALUE AND PRICE

Nearly all the elements of modern value and price theory figure in the writings of the Medieval Schoolmen. The conclusions of many contemporary writers generally contradict what was said by R. H. Tawney more than five decades ago: "The true descendant of the doctrines of Aquinas is the labour theory of value. The last of the schoolmen is Karl Marx."[1]

The concept of utility as a foundation of value is predominant in Western thought. Reference to this cause-and-effect relationship can be traced to the works of Greek authors. Xenophon wrote that "property is that which is useful for supplying a livelihood, and useful things turned out to be all those things that one knows how to use".[2] He also noted that "wealth is that from which a man can derive a profit".[3] For this disciple of Socrates, not even money is wealth to one who does not know how to use it.[4]

The Medieval Doctors derived their precepts in this regard from Aristotelian teachings. Since his terminology is subject to two possible translations, Aristotle's comments in this regard are the source of two currents of thought. In the *Nicomachean Ethics,* he used the Greek word *chreia,* which was usually translated into Latin as *indigentia*

---

[1] R. H. Tawney, *Religion and the Rise of Capitalism* (New York: Harcourt Brace, and Co., 1937), p. 36. Bernard W. Dempsey, Raymond De Roover, Marjorie Grice-Hutchinson, Emile Kauder and Joseph Höffner criticized Tawney's conclusion. See, for example, Raymond De Roover, "The Concept of the Just Price: Theory and Economic Policy", *Journal of Economic History* 18 (December 1958): 418–434.

[2] Xenophon, *Memorabilia and Oeconomicus,* English translation by E. C. Marchant (London: William Heinemann, 1923), p. 409.

[3] Ibid, p. 367.

[4] Ibid.

(need), although it can also be translated as *utilitas* or "use".[5] The Scholastics usually worked with the first translation, indicating that the price of goods does not depend on their nature but on the extent to which they serve the needs of mankind. Aristotle wrote that want is the cause and measure of human commerce. If no one needed the goods or labor of his fellows, men would cease to exchange their products.[6]

St. Augustine titled one chapter of his *City of God* "The distinctions among created things; and their different ranking by the scales of utility and logic". His remarks served as the starting point for Scholastic investigation of this issue. The Schoolmen studied the following passage in particular:

> Now among those things which exist in any mode of being, and are distinct from God who made them, living things are ranked above inanimate objects; those which have the power of reproduction, or even the urge toward it, are superior to those who lack that impulse. Among living things, the sentient rank above the insensitive, and animals above trees. Among the sentient, the intelligent take precedence over the unthinking—men over cattle. Among the intelligent, immortal beings are higher than mortals, angels being higher than men.
>
> This is the scale according to the order of nature; but there is another gradation which employs utility as the criterion of value. On this other scale we would put some inanimate things above some creatures of sense—so much so that if we had the power, we should be ready to remove these creatures from the world of nature, whether in ignorance of the place they occupy in it, or, through knowing that, still subordinating them to our own convenience. For instance, would not anyone prefer to have food in his house rather than fleas? There is nothing surprising in this; for we find the same

---

[5] Aristotle, *Nicomachean Ethics,* bk. V, chap. 5, para. 10–13 (1133a 26–28) English translation by H. Rackham (London: William Heinemann, 1947), p. 285. In many English editions *chreia* is translated as *demand:* "It is therefore necessary that all commodities shall be measured by some one standard, as was said before. And this standard is in reality demand."

[6] Ibid.

criterion operating in the value we place on human beings, for all the undoubted worth of a human creature. A higher price is often paid for a horse than for a slave, for a jewel than for a maidservant.

Thus there is a very wide difference between a rational consideration, in its free judgment, and the constraint of need, or the attraction of desire. Rational consideration decides on the position of each thing in the scale of importance, on its own merits, whereas need only thinks of its own interests. Reason looks for the truth as it is revealed to enlightened intelligence; desire has an eye for what allures by the promise of sensual enjoyment.[7]

From this, the Late Scholastics posited the idea that the value we place on goods depends on the utility we derive from them. Since our needs and desires are subjective, utility is subjective as well. In their discourses on value, St. Albert the Great, and later St. Thomas, included the element of "common estimation" (which was already present in the writings of the Roman jurist Paulus).[8]

Among the Schoolmen Olivi was the first to mention objective and subjective utility in relation to scarcity. Due to suspicion of heresy, his works were largely destroyed, so his discussions are not available in full. One of the few copies of his work that survived censorship bears the handwritten marginal comments of St. Bernardino.[9] In his own treatise, St. Bernardino stated that

> things have two values: one is natural [objective] and one is use based [mostly based on subjective utility]. Saleable goods are valued in the latter. And this use value [or value in use] can be considered from three perspectives:

[7] Saint Augustine, *City of God,* (London: Penguin, 1972), bk. XI, chap. 16, p. 447.

[8] "The prices of things function not according to the whim or utility of individuals, but according to the common estimate." *Corpus Iuris Civilis,* ed. Krueger-Mommsen (Berlin: Institutes, 1928), *Ad Legem Falcidiam, Digests,* XXXV, 2, 63, p. 556, quoted in B. W. Dempsey "Just Price in a Functional Economy". *American Economic Review* 25 (September 1935): 473–474.

[9] R. De Roover, *San Bernardino of Siena and Sant' Antonino of Florence—The Two Great Thinkers of the Middle Ages,* publication no. 19 of the Kress Library of Business and Economics (Cambridge, Mass.: 1967). See also De Roover, "The Concept of the Just Price", 418–434.

1) *Virtuositas* [Objective value in use]
2) *Raritas* [Scarcity]
3) *Complacibilitas* [Desirability][10]

In discussing the influence of *virtuositas* on prices, the Late Scholastics usually referred to the separate utilities that can be derived from similar products. It is for a different *virtuositas* that good wheat has a higher price than rotten wheat and that a good horse is valued more than one that is old and unproductive.[11]

St. Bernardino's explanation of the influence of scarcity on prices resolves the paradox of value:

> Water is usually cheap where it is abundant. But it can happen that, on a mountain or in another place, water is scarce, not abundant. It may well happen that water is more highly esteemed than gold, because gold is more abundant in this place than water.[12]

The third element, *complacibilitas,* was usually defined as similar to common estimation. The Schoolmen believed that the pleasure that people derive from different goods is subjective and arises from variable human opinion, so that "different people esteem goods differently".[13] What counts in determining prices, they avowed, is not particular *complacibilitas,* but common *complacibilitas.*

St. Antonino had basically the same theory of value. Perhaps because Francisco de Vitoria, who has been called the founding father of the Salamanca School and the Hispanic Scholastics, was very well acquainted with Antonino's *Summa,* his work exercised great influence on Late-Scholastic writings. All the other authors who influenced Vitoria (Conradus Summenhart, Sylvestre of Priero and Cajetan) shared similar points of view concerning the theory of value.[14] Cajetan's price theory is tained with subjective elements. He defines the just

[10] St. Bernardino of Siena, *Opera Omnia* (Venice, 1591), bk. II, Sermon XXXV, chap. 1, p. 335.

[11] Ibid.

[12] Ibid., bk. IV, Sermon XXX, p. 136.

[13] Ibid.

[14] An English translation of Antonino's writings on value appears in Dempsey, "Just Price in a Functional Economy". pp. 484–485.

price as that which is commonly paid "in a certain place and in a certain way of selling (on a public auction, through middlemen, etc.)".[15] This is why he concluded that if a house that is valued at 4,000 is sold for 1,000, "we say that the just price is one thousand as today no buyer was prepared to pay more".[16] Sylvestre analyzed estimation in detail,[17] and Conradus Summenhart included *virtuositas, raritas* and *complacibilitas* in his analysis.[18]

The Just Price Theory

Upon completing their discussions of value, the Schoolmen usually appended an analysis of price, sometimes treating value and price as synonyms and sometimes as slightly different terms. This creates some confusion, but generally speaking, it is proper to say that they deduced their price theory from their value theory. The Scholastic definition of just price was the price determined or established by common estimation in the market.[19] This definition had lasting influence. Writing 150 years later, Villalobos remarked:

> The value of things, which originates from common estimation, is not reduced by the knowledge of an individual. . . . The value which springs from abundance. . . . or a lack of merchandise, is extrinsic to the merchandise. It only varies its price through common estimation. It is worthwhile to know this.[20]

---

[15] Cajetan, *Commentarium in Summam Theologicam S. Thomae* (Lyon, 1568), qu. 77, p. 264.

[16] Ibid., p. 265.

[17] Sylvestre, *Summa Summarum quae Silvestrina dicitur,* bk. 1, s.v. *Estimatio* (Bolonia, 1514), p. 50.

[18] See p. 98, below.

[19] St. Bernardino, *Opera Omnia: "Secundum aestimationem fori ocurrentis, secundum quid tunc res, quae venditur, in loco illo communiter valere potest",* bk. II, Sermon xxxiii, p. 319.

[20] Henrique de Villalobos, *Summa de la Theologia Moral y Canónica,* (Barcelona, 1632), bk. II, p. 131.

Conradus Summenhart offered one of the most thorough analyses of the factors that influence prices. He listed

1. The abundance or superabundance of merchandise.
2. Accidental phenomena (such as plagues).
3. The ability and capacity (competence) of producers.[21]
4. The usefulness of the good (whether it can be used to produce other goods and how easy it is to transport).
5. The poverty of the region where the good is produced.
6. Scarcity (*raritas*). (He pointed out that even scarcity could cause variation in the prices of goods of the same nature or "nobility".)
7. *Complacibilitas.* (The desire for the good or the degree of pleasure which one can derive from the good).[22]
8. The counsel of righteous men.

Conradus presented the idea that the just price is not indivisible (there is not a *single just price*) and that things are worth as much as they can be licitly sold for.[23]

Francisco de Vitoria made similar statements:

It follows from this principle that wherever there is a marketable good for which there are many buyers and sellers, neither the nature of the good nor the price for which it was bought, that is to say, how expensive it was, nor the toil and trouble it was to get it should be taken into account *v.gr.* When Peter sells wheat, the buyer need not consider the money Peter spent nor his work, but rather, the common estimation of how much wheat is worth. If according to common estimation, the bushel of wheat is worth four silver pieces and somebody buys it for three, this would constitute an injustice to the seller because the common estimation of a bushel of wheat is

[21] He specifically stated that laziness should be expunged.

[22] Conradus employed arguments similar to those used by St. Bernardino and St. Antonino, to the effect that the desirability, or *complacibilitas,* that influences price is not individual but common. "The good that satisfies people more can be sold at a higher price than the one that satisfies people less" (n.p., 1515), *De Contractibus,* tractatus III, qu. LVI.

[23] *"Res tantum valet quantum licite posset vendi."* Ibid.

four silver pieces. In the same way, if that seller were to sell at a higher price, taking into account his expenses and his work, he would be selling unjustly, because *he should sell it according to the common estimation of the market.* About this topic you can read Conradus, in his treatise *Contractibus,* q. 56, conc. 1 and 2, where he formulates fifteen considerations that can be used to deduce the just price and just value of a good. But he also agrees that these considerations are valid and useful before the price of the good is established by the common estimation of men, because once the price is established in this way, it should be respected.[24]

After pointing out that the prices of goods that are different by nature (i.e., a table and a man) are influenced not by their essence but by common estimation and agreement, Vitoria repeated St. Augustine's and St. Thomas Aquinas' arguments concerning the value of animate things (which are higher in nature and lower in price) and inanimate things (lower in nature and sometimes higher in price). Stating that "when there are many buyers and sellers you must not take into consideration the nature of the thing, nor its cost", he added that "one must sell according to common estimation in the marketplace, at the market price [*a como vale en la plaza*]". Vitoria also applied this rule to goods that have many buyers and sellers, explaining that in this case the just price is the one resulting from "the common estimation of men excluding frauds and deceits". He specified that wheat, wine and cloth must be priced in this fashion. Although some analysts conclude that Vitoria was saying that the just price is equal to the market price in conditions of perfect competition,[25] one must exercise great care in jumping to this conclusion. "Perfect competition" is a mental construction that nowadays has a very special meaning. It requires a number of unrealistic assumptions. The Scholastic idea of competition was nearer to the "free-entry" assumption than to perfect-competition suppositions. Some modern economists argue that monopolies hinder perfect

---

[24] Francisco de Vitoria, *De Justitia* (Madrid: Publicaciones de la Asociación Francisco de Vitoria, 1934–1936), bk. 2, qu. 77, art. 1, pp. 117–118.

[25] For a modern analysis of this point see Luisa Zorraquín De Marcos, "An Inquiry into the Medieval Doctrine of the Just Price", master's thesis (Los Angeles: International College, 1984).

competition. According to the Late Scholastics, the price charged by a monopolist could, in certain cases, be a just price.[26] In the case of absence of competition, some Scholastics recommended the establishment of a legal price. Vitoria, Bañez, Medina and García, among others, prescribed cost-plus pricing in such cases.[27]

Borrowing some ideas from Conradus Summenhart's *De Contractibus,* Covarrubias declared that what must prevail in the establishment of just price is not the nature of the thing but human estimation alone, even if this estimation is insane.[28] Marjorie Grice-Hutchinson translated this passage as follows:

> The value of an article does not depend on its essential nature but on the estimation of men, even if that estimation be foolish. Thus, in the Indies, wheat is dearer than in Spain because men esteem it more highly, though the nature of the wheat is the same in both places.[29]

Luis de Molina composed one of the best summaries of Hispanic Scholastic just-price theory:

> In the first place, it should be observed that a price is considered just or unjust not because of the nature of the things themselves—this would lead us to value them according to their nobility or perfection—but due to their ability to serve human utility. Because this is the way in which they are appreciated by men, they therefore command a price in the market and in exchanges. Moreover, this is the end for which God gave things to man, and with that same end men divided among them the domain of all things, even though they belonged to everybody at the moment of their creation. What we have just

[26] See p. 119, below.

[27] Vitoria, *De Justitia,* p. 120; Juan de Medina, *De Contractibus* (Salamanca, 1550), qu. XXXI, fol. 92; Domingo de Bañez, *De Iustitia et Iure Decisiones* (Salamanca, 1594), p. 562; Francisco García, *Tratado Utilísimo de Todos los Contratos, Quantos en los Negocios Humanos se Pueden Ofrecer* (Valencia, 1583), p. 252; Pedro de Aragón, *De Iustitia et Iure* (Lyon, 1596), p. 437.

[28] *"Nec consitui iustum pretium ex natura rei: sed ex hominum aestimatione: tametsi insana sit aestimatio."* Diego Covarrubias y Leiva, *Opera Omnia* (Salamanca, 1577), bk. II, chap. III, p. 527.

[29] Marjorie Grice-Hutchinson, *Early Economic Thought in Spain,* 1177–1740 (London: Allen & Unwin, 1975), p. 100.

described explains why rats, which, according to their nature, are nobler than wheat, are not esteemed or appreciated by men. The reason is that they are of no utility whatsoever. This also explains why a house can be justly sold at a higher price than a horse and even a slave, even though the horse and the slave are, by nature, much nobler than the house.[30]

Molina's writings clearly reflect Augustinian reasonings. St. Augustine's theory could be interpreted as meaning that goods should be valued according their objective utility to satisfy human needs (rats would be of no value for men because, in essence, they are useless). If Molina's description had ended here, it would still be possible to argue that he had an objective theory of value. In the next paragraph, however, he explained that whenever he spoke of utility he was specifying subjective utility:

> In the second place, we should observe that the just price of goods is not fixed according to the utility given to them by man, as if, *caeteris paribus,* the nature and the need of the use given to them determined the quantity of price . . . it *depends on the relative appreciation which each man has for the use of the good.* This explains why the just price of a pearl, which can be used only to decorate, is higher than the just price of a great quantity of grain, wine, meat, bread or horses, even if the utility of these things (which are also nobler in nature) is more convenient and superior to the use of a pearl. That's why *we can conclude that the just price for a pearl depends on the fact that some men wanted to grant it value* as an object of decoration.[31]

In the case of pearls,

> It is evident that the price that is just for them comes neither from the nature of these things nor their utility, but from the fact that the Japanese took a liking to them and esteemed them in that way.[32]

---

[30] Luis de Molina, *La Teoría del Justo Precio* (Madrid: Ed. Nacional, 1981), pp. 167–168.

[31] Ibid., p. 168.

[32] Ibid. Utility was the essential element in Aragón's value theory. According to this author a good that had no utility (but had high production costs) cannot command a price. On the other hand, a good with high utility could command a price even when no expense was incurred. Molina, *De Iustitia et Iure* (Moguntiae, 1614), p. 180. He added that "all useful human acts deserve a price." Ibid., p. 182.

Juan de Lugo specified that even when human estimation seems ill-founded, it remains valid:

> Price fluctuates not because of the intrinsic and substantial perfection of the articles—since mice are more perfect than corn, and yet are worth less—but on account of their utility in respect of human need, and then only on account of estimation; for jewels are much less useful than corn in the house, and yet their price is much higher. And we must take into account not only the estimation of prudent men, but also of the imprudent, if they are sufficiently numerous in a place. This is why our glass trinkets are in Ethiopia justly exchanged for gold, because they are commonly more esteemed there. And among the Japanese old objects made of iron and pottery, which are worth nothing to us, fetch a high price because of their antiquity. Communal estimation, even when foolish, raises the natural price of goods, since price is derived from estimation. The natural price is raised by abundance of buyers and money, and lowered by the contrary factors.[33]

Explaining the relationship between human estimation and the value of things, Medina stated that the higher the esteem, *caeteris paribus,* the higher the value of the thing and vice versa.[34] In the same light, Francisco García determined that although the quality of the good influences the price, we should not confuse value with quality.

> This is manifest because we see variations in the prices of things which do not vary in quality: consider the example of a book. For one it is of great value and price; for another it is of low value and for others its value is nil. And the same thing happens with all products.[35]

"Prices reflect human opinion", because each person appreciates and esteems things in conformity with his view of their utility for human

---

[33] Quoted by Grice-Hutchinson, *Early Economic Thought,* pp. 101–102.

[34] The text in Latin reads: *"Tum etiam communis hominum estimatio & rerum appreciatio confert ad cognoscendum valorem rerum: & quo maior est aestimatio, ceteris paribus, maior est valor rerum: sicut e contra minor est valor, si minor sit hominum communia estimatio."* Medina, *De Contractibus,* p. 102.

[35] García, *Tratado Utilísimo,* p. 183.

service. García defined the quality of a good as "something intrinsic to the thing", while declaring that price "is extrinsic and depends on human esteem and judgment".[36] His point was that "human opinion determines prices entirely."[37]

These passages are clear and unambiguous. For the Schoolmen, value in exchange depends on value in use. Nonetheless, this value in use is not an objective quality. The Doctors found no objective way to establish the level of the just price, since utility is more closely related to the mood and preference of the consumer (*complacibilitas*) than to the inherent capacity of the good to satisfy human wants (*virtuositas*). For this reason the Scholastic utility theory of value must be understood as a subjective one. In effect, the Schoolmen were the forerunners of the late nineteenth-century economists who "discovered" the subjective theory of value.

Price Controls and Legal Price

In keeping with their theory that "so long as the transaction is *legal*, things are worth what they can be sold for", many Scholastics concluded that authority could place a legal price on some products, particularly in the case of a monopoly or when there were few buyers and sellers for a "very necessary good".[38] Some of the Schoolmen, however, opposed arbitrary price fixing and concluded that they would do more harm than good. Raymond De Roover summarized their point of view as follows:

> Later scholastics insisted that the just price was set by the community. This could be done in two ways: either by the chaffering of the market or by public decree. The latter was the legal price

---

[36] Ibid.
[37] Ibid., pp. 188–189.
[38] Vitoria, *De Justitia*, qu. 77, art. 1, p. 120.

as opposed to "the natural price", which was determined by "common estimation", i.e., by market valuation.[39]

To be just, however, the Schoolmen specified that the legal price should be *similar* to the market price.

The just natural price must be established by common estimation in the absence of fraud, force or monopolies. Both legal prices and natural prices thus derive from the just price. The Late Scholastics diagrammed this conclusion as follows:

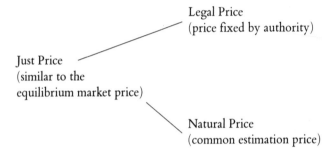

Legal Price
(price fixed by authority)

Just Price
(similar to the
equilibrium market price)

Natural Price
(common estimation price)

They recognized nonetheless that it is impossible to specify a *single* natural just price. Moralists may assign the qualification *just* to an entire range of prices. From the legal point of view, the Schoolmen considered this range to be very wide, while from the moral point of view it was more restricted. They stated that while it was legal for the seller to charge fifty percent more than the average just price, it was also legal for the buyer to pay less than fifty percent of the average price. Citing an example, Lessio postulated a just price of 10 for a certain good. From the legal point of view, the maximum price would be 15 and the minimum 5. From the moral point of view, the

---

[39] *New Catholic Encyclopedia*, s.v. "Scholastic Economics", by Raymond De Roover, vol. V, p. 68.

price might be 11 (the rigorous price), 10 (the medium price) and 9
(the infimum price):[40]

Moral point of view	Legal point of view
	Maximum price: 15
Rigorous price: 11	
Medium price: 10	Medium price: 10
Infimum price: 9	
	Minimum price: 5

Juan de Lugo noted that in the light of differing circumstances and
contributing factors, the majority of the Doctors agree that "it is
impossible to establish a rule."[41]

The Late Scholastics never questioned the right of the public
authorities to set a "fair" price,[42] but they questioned the convenience
of such price fixing. According to the Scholastic justification of
private property, it was *human law* that determined the ownership of a
specific good. The owner was free to use his goods at his will so long
as he did not exceed legal limitations. Human law also established the

---

[40] Leonardo Lessio, *De Iustitia et Iure* (Antwerp, 1626), p. 275. This explanation
can be considered as common doctrine. See Aragon, *De Iustitia,* p. 436, Antonio de
Escobar y Mendoza, *Universae Theologiae Moralis* (Lyon, 1662), p. 159, García,
Tratado Utilísimio, p. 240, Covarrubias, *Opera Omnia,* bk. II, chap. III, p. 524.
According to the Scholastics one could earn profit by selling the same good "at the
same place and at the same time" as long as the trading was done within the limits of
the "just" price (i.e., buying at the infimum and selling at the rigorous price).
García, p. 246.

[41] Juan de Lugo, *De Iustitia et Iure* (Lyon, 1670), bk. II, disp. XXVI, sect. IV, p. 279.

[42] De Roover, "The Concept of the Just Price", p. 425.

right of the state to restrict property use and possession. Taxes were the most clear example, constituting not only a restriction on the use of part of the property, but also an authoritarian confiscation of property to sustain "the whole" (the kingdom and its laws). Since the property the state takes away in the form of taxes is property that cannot be used at all, it was logical for the Schoolmen to reason that if the government had the right to confiscate property, it also had the right to restrict its use. This does not mean, however, that all the Late Scholastic authors declared that it was *convenient* for the prince to fix prices.[43]

For a legal price to be just, it had to take many things into consideration. Juan de Medina warned that from the seller's point of view (i.e., supply), the expenditures, work, care, industry and the risk and dangers inherent in transportation and storage must be prominent considerations. From the buyer's point of view (i.e., demand), the significant features were *complacibilitas, utilitas* and the number of prospective buyers. With regard to the good itself, the features of prime importance are scarcity, abundance, land fertility or sterility and whether the goods have deteriorated or improved. Medina concluded that when prices are fixed in this manner, not only will the prudent merchant recover his costs, but he should also be able to pay for his expenses, his work and his risks. Furthermore, he noted, none of these factors that can influence prices are static: they can and do change. Since expenditures, work and dangers may increase or decrease with time, time is a significant feature. The goods also change, either in nature (by getting better or worse) or in scarcity. The need for the good may fluctuate, and the number of buyers and sellers may also vary, as can human estimation of the good:

> As experience teaches, if you ask someone what the price of something is, one can say 10, others 12, but there are others who will oppose this, saying that the price is not 10 or 12, but 8 or 9.[44]

[43] De Roover stated that Martín de Azpilcueta opposed all price regulations and specified that "several others, among them Molina, looked upon price regulation with the same disfavor". Ibid., p. 426.

[44] Medina, *De Contractibus,* quaestio XXXI, *"De iusto rerum venalium precio",* pp. 88–89; Aragon explained the issue in the same words. *De Iustitia,* p. 438.

None of these factors can be deduced or established according to what happens to any one individual buyer or seller. It is not particular *complacibilitas* or individual esteem that counts, but *common estimation*. For this reason, the Medieval Schoolmen declared that it was legitimate to charge a high price (*"quantumcunque precium exigere"*) for bread in times of universal famine or to ask a very high price for medicine in times of universal plague.[45]

In this light, Medina criticized Duns Scotus' rule that prices should always cover costs.[46] Stating that common estimation need not consider the many costs incurred by the seller, he noted that it is one of the risks of the merchant (it is in the nature of "just" business) to be exposed to both profit and loss. In other words, Medina specified that "If you want to deal justly in business you have to realize that sometimes you are going to lose".[47] This does not mean that the seller is forbidden to use cost-plus pricing as a guide for establishing his prices. Medina declared it both licit and just, provided that the goods are *valued in utility* and *commonly esteemed* at the price the seller requires to cover his costs. Common estimation establishes just price. Since human estimation varies, there is no such thing as a *single* just price.

The Hispanic Scholastics realized the significance of common estimation in price determination and, therefore, its importance for profits. They also noted that, in the performance of their jobs, entrepreneurs and merchants incur considerable expenses which, in turn, may influence prices. Cajetan stated categorically that merchants "do not have to serve our comfort for free".[48]

Using the principle that "the king does not have the power (*potestas*) to do irrational and unjust things" as his basis, Molina criticized

---

[45] Medina, *De Contractibus,* pp. 88–89.

[46] "A person shall receive in the exchange recompense according to his diligence, prudence, trouble and risk." John Duns Scotus (1265–1308), *Opera Omnia* (Paris, 1894), vol. 18, "Quaestiones in Quartum Librum Sententiarum", dist. XV, quaestio 2a, nn. 22–23, quoted in Dempsey "Just Price", pp. 483–484.

[47] The text in Latin reads: *"Si iuste res suas vendere volunt, aliquando lucrari, aliquando perdere: talis est ipsorum mercatorum conditio, ut sicut lucro, ita & damno se exponant."* Ibid., p. 95.

[48] Tomas de Vío (Cajetan), qu. 77, p. 267.

arbitrary price fixing. He posited a situation involving a great scarcity of wheat and predicted that if the prince expected the wheat to be sold at the same price as in times of abundance, he would fix an irrational, unjust price.

> And it must not be said that this action is correct because it is convenient for the common good that the wheat be sold at the same price in times of scarcity and in times of abundance; and that acting in this way the poor will not be burdened and they will find it easy to buy wheat. . . . I insist that this is not reasonable.[49]

In the first place, Molina invoked the common good. If justice and equity require a price increase that will, incidentally, hurt the poor, their interests must be protected by other means: "they must be helped with alms rather than with sales [meaning maximum prices]".[50] His second point is that when high prices threaten the poor, it would be unjust to punish the seller by setting prices below the just minimum. In fact, such an action would not help the poor,

> especially because we know that in times of scarcity and hunger the poor can rarely buy the wheat at the official price. On the contrary, the only ones who can buy at that price are the powerful and the public ministers [public servants], because the owner of the wheat cannot resist their requests.[51]

Third, Molina added that the cost of what the republic demands for the common good must be borne collectively by all citizens. "And it would be unjust to place the burden upon the owners of the wheat only." His fourth point was that in times of scarcity, the farmer usually has to undertake large expenditures, and the fixed legal price generally does not allow him to recover his costs. According to Molina, this violates equity.

Molina reasoned that farmers would suffer great damage if the state controlled the price of wheat while allowing the price of other products to increase or decline in response to changes in supply and

---

[49] Molina, *De Iustitia,* disputa CCCLXIV, point 3, pp. 383–384.

[50] Ibid.

[51] Ibid., p. 384.

demand. His entire analysis posited the existence of a natural price that would be very similar in nature to the natural price defined by the classical economists of the nineteenth century. He spoke of a natural just price that not even the law could change. Molina emphasized that in times of scarcity men were not obliged to sell at the price fixed by the authority in times of abundance, because they could suppose that it was not the will of the prince that a law enacted in times of abundance should have equal power in times of scarcity. If, on the other hand, such "is in the will of the prince, the law would be unjust and unreasonable, so it would not oblige in conscience".[52]

Mariana shared the same point of view. Citing many reasons and basing his deductions on both past and present experience, he announced that price controls were extremely inappropriate and harmful.[53] Martín de Azpilcueta declared that according to the opinion of all the Doctors, an unjust official price "does not oblige". Since an unjust official price can be the cause of many mortal sins, people do not sin by selling "their goods at the price that is just in God's presence, although it exceeds the official price". For him, natural justice was the only limit.[54]

Villalobos cited logical reasons for his opposition to price fixing:

> I think it would be better not to have an official price (*tassa*) for wheat, as happens in many places without detrimental effects. Rebelo says that everyone in Lisbon would have died of hunger if an official wheat price had been established. The reason for what I say, as we can see, is that in cheap years the maximum price is useless. The same is true of average years, because the value [price] of wheat doesn't reach the maximum price, and the price is reduced or raised according to the existent abundance. In expensive years, despite the fixed price, the price rises for one reason or another, and you will not find a single grain of wheat at the official price . . . and if you do find it, it will be with a thousand cheats and frauds. And also because it seems a harmful thing to oblige the farmers to sell at the official price in

---

[52] Ibid., pt. 4, p. 385.

[53] See p. 83n.

[54] Martín de Azpilcueta, *Manual de Confesores y Penitentes* (Salamanca, 1556), pp. 476–477; Aragón, *De Iustitia,* p. 435.

wheat-scarce years, when they have to pay high production costs and when common estimation grants a higher price to wheat.[55]

For many Late Scholastics, laws establishing prices for goods had no absolute value. Villalobos declared that in times of scarcity, one is not, in good conscience, obliged to sell at the official price. He noted general agreement on this point:

> Juan de Medina, Navarro, Rebelo, Molina all say this, and Ledesma states that members of the Jesuit order ascribe to this opinion. It is based on the fact that in order for the price to be just, it must be reasonable, and it wouldn't be so if it were notably less than the valuation of the good made by common estimation. And this is what is happening now.[56]

To assure "equality" in the price, common estimation should establish the just price; otherwise, "the owners of the wheat would suffer a great damage". Villalobos then quoted Molina:

> If, when a great scarcity appears, the prince wants the wheat to be sold at a price that would be reasonable in times of abundance, the law would be irrational and unjust.[57]

Here again, this Franciscan author determined that the prince cannot justify his price by saying that it is "for the common good". Villalobos followed Molina's arguments quite closely,[58] also admitting that such judgments in economic problems are matters of opinion:

[55] Villalobos, *Summa,* p. 344.

[56] Ibid., p. 347.

[57] The Latin text reads: *"Si superveniente ingente sterilitate Princeps vellet, ut triticum pretio venderetur, qui rationabiliter tempore abundantie vendebatur, lex esset irrationabilis, et iniusta."* Ibid.

[58] The prince cannot justify himself by saying that it is convenient to "sell the wheat at the same price in times of scarcity so the poor will be able to acquire it. . . . In conformity with the nature of things, equity (sp. *equidad*) and justice may demand a rise in its price (so that the owner of the wheat does not suffer an injustice). One must not take into consideration that coincidentally it will be very difficult for the poor to buy the wheat. This can be resolved through alms. One cannot oblige all the sellers to sell at that price in order to help the poor. Moreover, in times of scarcity and hunger, the poor seldom buy at the official price [tassa]. Ibid.

Anyone can follow the one he wants, especially the one that has more foundation, because it will be more probable.[59]

Prices and Equality

To judge whether there was justice in a transaction, the Schoolmen had to determine if the transaction had been undertaken and completed voluntarily. They frequently quoted Aristotle's dictum "nobody suffers injustice voluntarily,"[60] and their price theory followed the same reasoning.[61] Vitoria clarified that justice and legality in exchange

> are based on a universal and certain principle and this is that I am not obliged to benefit and please my neighbor gratis and without a profit, even when I could do so with no cost or work. (If he begs me to dance, I say I do not want to if you don't give me a ducat, and I can say the same thing in all other cases).[62]

Vitoria allowed two exceptions: spiritual benefits[63] and *mutuum* (loans). Each person is the judge and moderator of his property.[64] Villalobos noted that it goes against justice and reason to oblige someone to "pay a price for something which does not interest him".[65] If someone undertakes a transaction, by definition he does so voluntarily. For Albornóz, equality in transactions occurs only in the absence of coercion,

> because so long as they make someone sell his property by force, it does not matter if they give him a price ten times higher than its value [current price], they are not giving him its value, because he

[59] Ibid., p. 348.
[60] *"Volenti non fit injura." Nicomachean Ethics,* 1138a, 13–14.
[61] E.g., Medina, *De Contractibus,* p. 97.
[62] Francisco de Vitoria, *Opera Omnia* (Salamanca, 1952), vol. VI, p. 514.
[63] Priests are obliged to give certain spiritual goods to those who demand them (for instance, confessions and communions).
[64] *"In re sua quilibet est moderatur & arbiter."*
[65] Villalobos, *Summa,* p. 407.

will esteem his property more than the price that they are giving him. In this way the price is not equal to the thing (and as we have seen, justice in prices consists of this). The same happens in the buying process if they force someone to buy something he doesn't want, although they give him the object for ten times less than its value.[66]

The Late Scholastics deemed a sale involuntary whenever it took place in the context of violence, fraud or ignorance.[67] García specified that violence could be explicit or implicit. When a judge ruled that a defendant should relinquish his property as restitution for proven wrongs, he was enacting explicit violence for the purpose of justice. García characterized unjust perpetration of explicit violence as that which originates from private action rather than the judicial system. Implicit violence, he avowed, may take the form of monopoly (state-imposed privilege for one seller, which prevents others from selling) or cornering the market (which prevents others from buying). García stipulated that by definition both forms of implicit violence are unjust.[68] He declared that fraud renders a sale involuntary, be it fraud regarding the substance, the quantity or the quality of a product. Ignorance relates to substance, quantity and quality as well. García outlined his theory as follows:[69]

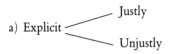

a) Explicit —— Justly / Unjustly

1) Violence

b) Implicit —— Monopoly / Cornering

---

[66] Bartolome de Albornóz, *Arte de los Contratos* (Valencia, 1573), p. 69.
[67] García, *Tratado Utilisimo,* p. 368.
[68] Ibid., p. 375.
[69] Ibid., p. 379.

	a) In substance
2) Fraud	b) In quantity
	c) In quality

	a) Of the substance
3) Ignorance	b) Of the quantity
	c) Of the quality

In contracts, García explained,

> Both the buyer and the seller benefit [receive utility] because the latter needs the former's money and the former needs a commodity. For this reason, each of these things is given as a reward for the other.[70]

The Schoolmen decreed that coercion, violence, misrepresentation and inadequate information all undermine equality in a transaction. Therefore they do not serve justice. Equality is served when each participant receives parallel utility. Many historians believe that the concept of "reciprocity in exchange" constitutes the essence of Scholastic price theory. In Aristotelian thought, "reciprocity in exchange" prevails when both parties enjoy the same wealth after an exchange as before it. In St. Thomas Aquinas' words, "any exchange is for the mutual benefit of both parties with the result that they are better off than previously".[71]

Soto interpreted Aristotle's term "reciprocity of exchange" as the idea that justice is not achieved when one merely exchanges one good for another (i.e., shoes for a home), but when one gives enough shoes

---

[70] Ibid., p. 213.

[71] St. Thomas Aquinas, *Summa Theologica* (London: Blackfriars, 1975), II–II, qu. 77, art 1, resp. Reciprocity in exchange can be better understood from the accountant's perspective. In the exchange of cash (an asset) for goods (another asset), the only thing that appears at first on the balance sheet is a change from liquid assets (cash) to inventory assets. This does not alter the total assets. The situation is similar to what it was before the transaction.

to equal the price of the house, because goods do not have the same value (price).[72] Albornóz explained that the seller's wealth should be increased by the same amount as the buyer's. This amount is equivalent to the price.[73] A price is therefore just when it preserves equality.

Donation

Donations play an important role in the Scholastic understanding of economics. Any person who has the perfect ownership of a good can give it freely to another.[74] Since the owner of a thing is also owner of its use, he can transfer the thing itself or its use.[75] Gifts, i.e., liberal transfers or alms, are essential elements in Christian ethics. St. Bernardino defines donation as the liberal act of the person who transfers a good without expecting something in return.[76] In the context of donation, the problem of just price cannot arise. Neither utility nor equality are pertinent.

The Schoolmen stipulated that a buyer who deliberately and knowingly pays a price that greatly exceeds the usual market price has added a donation to the transaction. When he does so freely, such *donationis admixtae* is perfectly legitimate. Juan de Medina determined that when the buyer pays an excessive price, and it is his intention to

---

[72] Domingo de Soto, *De Iustitia et Iure* (Madrid: IEP, 1968) bk. VI, qu. 6.

[73] *"Porque tanto entra con el precio en poder del vendedor, quanto por la cosa vendida en poder del comprador, quanto por el precio que salió de su caudal, y tanto entra por la cosa vendida en poder de el comprador, quanto por el precio salio de su caudal,"* Albornóz, *Arte,* p. 63.

[74] Imperfect ownership, such as the domain a priest exercises over Church property, does not involve this right. Children who have not yet reached the age of reason also exercise imperfect domain.

[75] García, *Tratado Utilísimo,* p. 213.

[76] *"Per actum mere liberalem (quando transferos nullam expectat redditionem)."* St. Bernardino, *Opera Omnia,* Sermon XXXII, art. 3.

donate that amount freely, we cannot speak of a pure sale.[77] Medina elaborated three specific regulations regarding donations:

1. The buyer must be an intelligent person (sagacious), with knowledge of the market price of the thing.
2. There should be no suspicion that the seller lied about the price of the commodity.
3. The buyer must not be in grave need of the good in question.[78]

In such cases, it is legal to sell at a price that exceeds the limits of the just price.

Prices and Knowledge

Although the Late Scholastics argued that ignorance could render an exchange involuntary, they also reasoned that it was licit to profit from one's own knowledge as well as the ignorance of others. The unknowing sale of a faulty product, for example, would not constitute fraud, yet the buyer could claim that it was not his will to buy the product in that state.

To prove that profit derived from knowledge of the market is legitimate, the Schoolmen usually repeated St. Thomas Aquinas' example of a merchant who, knowing that there was going to be a future increase in the supply of a good, sold his inventory before the new goods arrived on the market. They also cited Genesis 41, where an informed Joseph advised the pharaoh to "stock up" in preparation for bad times. The pharaoh then grew rich buying at a low price and

---

[77] "*Sit, quando ipse emens dat precium excesivum, cuius excessum donare libere intendit: quia tunc non est venditio & emptio pura, sed mixta donationi, rationi cuius licitum est venditori illum excessum recipere in his casibus est licitum rem vendere pro precio excedente latitudinem iusti pretii.*" Medina, *De Contractibus,* p. 98.

[78] Pedro de Aragón shared the same view, and for him, one could presume donation when the buyer was not impelled by need. Aragón quoted Diego Covarrubias y Leiva as saying: "*Quod quando nulla necessitate coactus quis emit orem pro maior pretio, commode praesumitur donare.*" Aragon, *De Iustitia,* lib. 2, chap. 4, n. 11.

selling at a higher price.[79] The Scholastics ruled that knowledge should not be penalized. They further noted that the knowledge or ignorance of one man does not change "the just price". It is abundance or scarcity in the market that does that. An individual may acquire special knowledge of future shipments, supplies, legislation or variations in the value of money. Even when such influential factors are already in operation, if the public remains unenlightened, the knowledgeable seller may employ his information to make a profit. Lessio reasoned that if justice does not permit knowledgeable sellers to command the current price,

> buyers, following the same reasoning, should not be allowed to buy at the current price if they know that prices in the future will go up, and this is also false.[80]

Monopoly Theory

Many of the Late Scholastic Doctors studied the issue of monopoly in combination with the problem of just price. Miguel Salón and Luis de Molina[81] defined monopoly by its etymological roots: the word *monos* (from the Latin meaning *one*), and the word *polium* (from the Greek *pola,* which means *sale*). Molina reasoned that in a stricter sense, monopoly exists when "one or more persons obtain an exclusive privilege to sell a certain good".[82] Although this definition implies that monopolies derive from privileges, and privileges can be granted only by authority, the Schoolmen also spoke of other monopolistic activities. Lessio distinguished four types of monopoly: those formed through

---

[79] *"Vili pius emendo, & care postea vendendo Pharaonem ditavit."* Ibid., p. 454. Lessio, *De Iustitia,* p. 279.

[80] *"Alioquin emptor non posset emere pretio currente, si sciret pretium postea valde augendum, quod tamen falsum esse . . . Abundantia praessens vel inminiens facit decrescere pretium, si passim sciatur; secus si ignoretur, non decrescit pretium unde potes tuas pretio antiquo eatenus usitato vendere."* Ibid.

[81] Miguel Salón, *Commentariorum in Disputationem de Iustitia* (Valencia, 1591), p. 1992. Molina, *De Iustitia,* disp. CCCXLV.

[82] Ibid.

conspiracy, those enacted by the prince, those accomplished by cornering the market and those resulting from import restrictions.[83] Either entrepreneurs or workers could engage in conspiracy to establish a monopoly. The Schoolmen criticized them both. They specifically denounced pacts among artisans that the work started by one would not be completed by another or agreements that they would refuse to work except for a predetermined wage.[84]

The Scholastics considered monopolies established by public authority to be justifiable if they were for the benefit of the republic. Citing as an example the benefits that accrue to the republic from the labors of writers and printers, they approved what modern legislation terms *copyright laws.* Lessio specified that when the prince has good reason, he may grant exclusive privileges.[85] In this case, prudent judgment based on thorough study of the circumstances, should help to identify the just price.[86] Molina justified some monopolies created with the permission of the prince, saying that "if the king can ask his subjects to contribute . . . for a public need, he can also impose upon them the burden of a monopoly, so long as this burden is moderate".[87]

In the field of economic ethics, Molina reasoned that the king or the republic that grants privileges in a way that harms its subjects is committing a mortal sin, as are those who ask for such privileges or make use of them. Such privileges violate the consumers' right to buy from the cheapest seller. They also violate the rights of other potential suppliers. Molina therefore concluded that both the prince and those who benefit from the privilege are obliged to offset the damage caused to buyers and sellers.[88] While Ledesma stated that "many monopolies

---

[83] Lessio, *De Iustitia,* p. 295.

[84] Escobar, *Theologia Moralis,* p. 163: *"quando venditores conspirant inter se de pretio: tunc modo id non sit supra legitimum vel supra vulgare summum non peccant contra iustitiam, quamuis bene contra charitatem, secus si pretium sit supra legitimum, tunc enim restitutionem illius auctuarii tenentur."*

[85] Lessio, *De Justitia,* p. 295; De Roover, "The Concept of the Just Price", p. 427.

[86] Bañez, *De Iustitia,* p. 538; Escobar wrote that *"hoc monopolium est licitum modo iustum pretium mercibus a Principe sit taxatum". Theologia Moralis,* p. 163.

[87] Molina, *De Iustia,* disp. CCCXLV.

[88] Ibid.

exist in this way",[89] Lessio added that monopolies created by the prince and not needed for the common good or those that grant iniquitous privileges will harm the citizens, limiting their freedom without benefiting the republic.[90] Mariana also condemned monopolies established by the prince without the people's consent. According to him, the prince lacked legitimate authority to conscript part of the property of his subjects in an unjust manner.[91]

The Schoolmen sometimes accused those who buy up the entire supply of a certain good as being monopolists who *cornered the market,* but Aragón explained that they are not unjust if they assume the risk of buying the goods without committing fraud and without the intention of increasing prices. Antonio de Escobar shared that same opinion.[92]

In their discussion of *import restrictions,* the Late Scholastics reasoned as do many contemporary free-market economists. Not only do monopolies formed by means of restricted imports damage those tradesmen who could have imported the goods, but they also damage the community through higher prices. Antonio de Escobar condemned those who impede an increase in the supply of goods by restricting

---

[89] Pedro de Ledesma, *Summa* (Salamanca, 1614), p. 518.

[90] This author adopted a different attitude toward monopolies of necessities and those of "luxuries". Raymond De Roover pointed out: "If it applies to necessities, the prince ought to be extremely careful to keep the price low but, if trifles or luxuries are involved, he may have good cause to make them expensive and to restrict consumption." "Monopoly Theory Prior to Adam Smith: A Revision", *Quarterly Journal of Economics* 65 (May 1951): 500. Lessio's Latin text reads: *"secus tamen si id concedat in mercibus, quae solum ad delicias & luxum pertinent, quas nemo cogitur emere, ut sunt picturae, varia genera tapetium, sericorum, pannorum, & holosericorum, oleo, fritilli, chartulae lusoriae, latrunculi & similia. Cum enim in his nemo gravetur, nisi qui sponte vult, (nisi forte pauci aliqui divites) facile potest princps habere iustam causam non impediendi ne iustum pretium excedant." De Justitia,* p. 295.

[91] Juan de Mariana, *Del Rey y de la Institución Real,* in *Biblioteca de Autores Espagñoles,* Rivadeneyra, vol. 31 (Madrid: Editions Atlas, 1950), p. 579.

[92] Escobar, *Theologia Moralis,* p. 163, and Aragón, *De Iustitia,* p. 463. The latter text reads: *"Caeterum, si ille, qui totam mercium quantitatem emit, nec cum aliquo fraudulenter convenit, nec animo. Pretium ultra iustum augendi, id fecit, sed suo pericula illas accipiens, nullam iniquitatem committet."*

imports.[93] Azplicueta, Salón, Aragón and Bonacina all spoke to this subject.

In each of these areas, the Schoolmen rarely criticized monopoly *per se.* The existence of a solitary seller was not enough to prove either that the prince was unjust or that the monopolist had achieved his position through special privilege or by means of fraud or deceit.[94] Pedro de Aragón avowed that a monopoly is not unjust if it buys and sells at just prices. He did, however, criticize those who acquire monopolistic power by impeding the importation of foreign goods, stating that such merchants err in placing their private utility before public utility.[95]

[93] Ibid., p. 163.
[94] Salón, *Commentariorum,* col. 1992.
[95] Aragón, *De Iustitia,* p. 463.

8

DISTRIBUTIVE JUSTICE

Most of the economic reasonings of the Medieval Schoolmen appear in their treatises on justice and law (*De Iustitia et Iure*) and in their books on moral theology. The issue of justice, however, figures in nearly every analysis they made. In general, they followed the teachings of Aristotle and St. Thomas Aquinas.

As did Aristotle, St. Thomas postulated two forms of justice:

> In the first place there is the order of one part to another, to which corresponds the order of one private individual to another. This order is directed by commutative justice, which is concerned about the mutual dealings between two persons. In the second place there is the order of the whole toward the parts, to which corresponds the order of that which belongs to the community in relation to each single person. This order is directed by distributive justice, *which distributes common goods proportionately.* Hence there are two species of justice, distributive and commutative.[1]

Noting that this definition of distributive justice is consistent with the principle of justice in general, i.e., "to render to each one his right", he continued:

> Even as part and whole are somewhat the same, so too that what pertains to the whole, pertains somewhat to the part also: so that when the goods of the community are distributed among a number of individuals each one receives that which, in a way, is his own.[2]

It is important to note that in the Thomist tradition, distributive justice refers only to common goods. Furthermore, St. Thomas distinguished between public common goods and common goods belong-

---

[1] St. Thomas Aquinas, *Summa Theologica* (London: Blackfriars, 1975), II–II, qu. 61, art. 1.

[2] Ibid., qu. 61, art. 2.

ing to a family or to other groups of people. Since "the act of distributing the goods of the community belongs to none but those who exercise authority over those goods",[3] he indicated that the charge of distributing public common goods falls to governmental authorities, bureaucrats or anyone charged with their care or provision. The "subjects" are also responsible for distributive justice "in so far as they are contented by a just distribution".[4]

Aristotelian, Thomist and Scholastic thought provided that just distribution of common goods involves proportionate allocation. St. Thomas noted that

> in distributive justice something is given to a private individual, in so far as what belongs to the whole is due to the part, and in a quantity that is proportionate to the importance of the position of that part in respect of the whole. Consequently, in distributive justice a person receives all the more of the common goods, according as he holds a more prominent position in the community. This prominence in an aristocratic community is gauged according to virtue, in an oligarchy according to wealth, in a *democracy according to liberty,* and in various ways according to various forms of government.[5]

Luis de Molina reasoned similarly:

> Distributive justice refers precisely to what is owed to someone because he belongs to a community, in which case common goods must be divided among the members (something that seldom occurs). And since a republic is a collection of members, it is evident that its goods belong to its members, who own them in common. If they come to be overabundant, they should be distributed and divided among the members of the republic, and each should receive a share.[6]

Some lines later, he defined this kind of justice as that which "gives each member of the republic what belongs to him when the common

---

[3] Ibid.
[4] Ibid.
[5] Ibid., II–II, qu. 61, art. 3. [Italics mine.]
[6] Luis de Molina, *De Iustitia et Iure* (Moguntiae, 1614), bk. 1, col. 24.

goods are divided according to geometric proportion".[7] It appears that, for Molina, it was rare for common goods or the surplus of a common good to be divided among the citizens ("something that seldom occurs"). In his experience the opposite is the norm: the citizens are obliged to maintain common goods.

While distributive justice takes place in the context of the relationship between the state and the people, "*commutative* justice directs *commutations* that can take place between two persons".[8] Late Scholastic theory analyzed profits, wages and rent as matters of commutative justice and applied rules similar to those used to analyze the prices of goods. The Schoolmen determined that wages, profits and rents are not for the government to decide. Since they are beyond the sphere of distributive justice, they should be determined through common estimation in the market.[9]

---

[7] Ibid.

[8] Aquinas, *Summa,* II–II, qu. 61, art. 3.

[9] For a more detailed analysis see Alejandro A. Chafuen, "Justicia Distributiva en La Escolastica Tardia", *Estudios Publicos* 18 (1985).

9

WAGES

The Medieval Schoolmen declared wages to be a question of commutative justice. They usually devoted a chapter of their treatises on rent (*locatione*)[1] to this issue. It was natural and consistent for them to analyze the buying and selling of all productive factors (including the hiring of laborers) in conjunction with their study of prices. Luis de Molina argued that

> in addition to renting his belongings and the things someone gave him to rent, one can also hire himself out to render a service to another, i.e., teaching, defending *people* in court or for many other services and functions.[2]

The tradition of treating wages as a matter of commutative justice similar to the exchange of other economic goods can be traced to St. Thomas Aquinas, who stated that wages are the natural remuneration for labor "almost as if it were the price of the same" (*Quasi quoddam pretium ipsius*).[3] St. Bernardino applied the same tenets to wages as to prices. His contemporary, St. Antonino, did likewise, offering detailed analyses of the specific problems associated with many different jobs.[4] As Raymond De Roover correctly pointed out, his position is some-

---

[1] *Locatione* is usually translated as "hiring and letting". See Samuel Pufendorf, *De Jure Naturae et Gentium Libri Octo,* edited by James Brown Scott (London: Oceana, 1934) p. 741.

[2] Luis de Molina, *De Iustitia et Iure* (Moguntiae, 1614), disp. 486, col. 1064.

[3] St. Thomas Aquinas, *Summa Theologica* (London: Blackfriars, 1975), I–II, qu. 114, art. 4, resp.

[4] St. Antonino had a great knowledge of the different jobs that existed in fourteenth-century Florence. He discussed, among others, the wages of lawyers, medical doctors, merchants and textile workers. *Summa Theologica* (Lyon, 1516), III, Titulo VI, § IIII.

what more "liberal" than that of St. Thomas Aquinas.[5] While Aquinas declared that wages are *almost* the same as prices, St. Antonino omitted the *almost.* Villalobos dealt with salaries in his chapter on hiring. He believed that in matters of wages, "we have to judge in the same way as we judge the just price of other saleable goods".[6]

According to the Schoolmen, supply, demand and cost are not the only operative factors in wage determination. Sylvestre noted in his *Summa* that the estimation of a good reflects appreciation of it. If it is a productive good (*rei fructuosa*), he added, its price should depend on the revenue (*reditus*) it can produce.[7] In effect, Sylvestre posited an implicit imputation theory.[8]

The "Just Wage"

In the field of labor, the question of just wages and salaries was the most important problem the Schoolmen faced. To address this issue, they first explained how prices and wages are determined in the market. Their *theory of wages* is perfectly consistent with their price theory.

Luis de Molina's writings on salaries exerted great influence on other authors and thus have been the object of extensive study by twentieth-century historians. St. Bernardino and St. Antonino had preceded him in these ideas.

St. Antonino demonstrated great knowledge of the labor market in the textile industry and used clear logic in his exposition of the just wage as the wage established by common estimation in the absence of

---

[5] Raymond De Roover, *San Bernardino of Siena and Sant' Antonino of Florence, Two Great Economic Thinkers of the Middle Ages* (Cambridge, Mass.: Kress Library, 1967), p. 24.

[6] Henrique de Villalobos, *Summa de la Theologia Moral y Canónica* (Barcelona, 1632), p. 397.

[7] Sylvestre de Priero, *Sylvestrinae Summae* (Antwerp, 1578), s.v. *"Estimatio".*

[8] The Austrian school of Economics employs this theory to explain means-of-production value. For a detailed discussion of this matter see pp. 183–184, below.

fraud.[9] Luis Saravia de la Calle followed the tradition of St. Bernardino and St. Antonino, warning that we must analyze "the just wage of laborers, journeymen, officials and others"[10] with the same scrutiny and logic we devote to the pricing of commodities.

According to Molina, a proper wage reflects the salary normally paid for similar jobs in similar circumstances:

> After considering the service that an individual undertakes and the large or small number of people who at the same time are found in similar service, if the wage that is set for him is at least the lowest wage that is customarily set in that region at that time for people in such service, the wage is to be considered just.[11]

Underlining the voluntary nature of all contracts, he rejected the idea that wages should be based on the workers' need:

> Unless it is wholly clear in the light of all attendant circumstances that the agreed-upon wage violates the limits of the *infimum* just price and for that reason is clearly unjust, we must not consider this wage as unjust, not only according to civil law, but also in conscience. For this reason, the servant cannot demand something more, or if he does not receive it, secretly appropriate the goods of his master in reward for his service. And if he surreptitiously takes something, if we can presuppose that it is against the will of the master, ... he commits theft and is obliged to make restitution. This is true even though the servant may barely support himself and live a miserable life with this salary, because the owner is only obliged to pay him the just wage for his services considering all the attendant circumstances, *not what is sufficient for his sustenance and much less for the maintenance of his children and family.*[12]

Molina defined the *infimum just price* of labor as the lowest wage determined by common estimation. A wage is legal if it falls somewhere between 50 percent above or below the just wage. Only when

---

[9] St. Antonino, *Summa Theologica* (Lyon: Johannis Cleyn, 1516), pt. III, titulo 8, chap. 2.

[10] Luis Saravia de la Calle, *Instrucción de Mercaderes* (Madrid, 1949), p. 55.

[11] Molina, *De Iustitia,* bk. 2, dis. 506, col. 1146. See also Villalobos, *Summa,* p. 407.

[12] Molina, *De Iustitia,* col. 1147.

a salary constitutes less than half the just wage will the employer be obliged to compensate the laborer for the difference. To prove that a wage is just, one must not consider the needs of the laborer or his subsistence level, but rather, the wages normally paid for similar jobs in similar circumstances. Molina stated that this reasoning can be generalized in reference to any kind of job, be it public or private. "This is evident because when it is not clear that the contract is unjust one must stick to it and what was agreed by both parties must be considered just."[13] He added that

> this stipend may not be sufficient for the full support of themselves or their families. Many, however, freely take up these employments for the stipulated wage because, although it does not provide for complete sustenance, it helps and becomes sufficient with the other resources that the individuals who take the employment at this wage may have and with the labor they can devote to other tasks; and when many are found who willingly undertake this service for the given wage, the wage is not to be considered an unjust payment for that service or task because it is paid to an individual for whom it does not afford a living because he lacks other resources or employment, or because he has many children, or because he wishes to live at a higher standard, or with a larger household than he would otherwise live.[14]

The common estimation wage was subject to the influence of supply and demand, which had to be taken into account together with the absence of force or fraud and the fulfillment of the contract. The voluntary nature of the labor contract is an important point in Late Scholastic theory. Writing some years before Molina, Soto stipulated that "if they freely accepted this salary for their job, it must be just".[15] Furthermore, they may not claim "insufficient wages" as justification for pilfering:

[13] Ibid.

[14] Ibid. Translation from *New Catholic Encyclopedia,* vol. V, p. 52.

[15] Domingo de Soto, *De Iustitia et Iure* (Madrid: IEP, 1968) bk. V, qu. III, art. 3, fol. 150.

Under no circumstance can servants, be they of the king or of inferior lords, surreptitiously take something from their masters with the excuse that they are not sufficiently well paid.[16]

This is especially true when the servants have freely accepted that salary "because no injury is done to those who gave their consent". For this reason, he advised them, "if you do not want to serve for that salary, leave!"[17]

The Franciscan priest Villalobos criticized those laborers who wanted to legislate their own "justice". He refuted their arguments as follows:

And when they [the laborers] say that the wage is below the just minimum, it seems we cannot believe them, because if they could find another [employer] who would pay them more, they would go and work for him, but as they cannot find one, they are like goods that one [the potential buyer] has to beg [to purchase]. . . . For that reason they have a lower value because the services are worth less when there is a dearth of employers, as are goods when there is a lack of buyers. . . . So they have nothing to complain about.[18]

Employers may refuse to hire labor when the price is very high since "it is against reason and justice to want someone to buy or hire at a price he does not want."[19]

For Lessio, not even the wages of those who worked for the republic (the state) could be treated as a problem of distributive justice.[20] As did Molina, Lessio wrote that a salary is just if it is similar to what is customarily paid, as long as it remains within the limits of the just price. If a salary sometimes falls below the infimum just price, he noted, one must be careful not to judge too hastily, because many people may freely and voluntarily agree to that salary. Furthermore, wages do not consist of a monetary amount alone. Salaries can be very low, but when they include honor, Lessio re-

---

[16] Ibid.

[17] *"Et ideo si non vis illo pretio servire, abi."* Ibid.

[18] Villalobos, *Summa,* p. 407.

[19] Ibid.

[20] Leonardo Lessio, *De Iustitia et Iure* (Antwerp, 1626) bk. II, chap. 24, d. IV, p. 326.

minded his readers, the distinction functions as a part of the salary.[21]

A legal salary may also fall below the infimum level when there is no agreement that any salary must indeed be paid, or when the payment is left to the will of the lord. According to most of the Schoolmen, the equitable thing to do in this case is to pay a sum similar to the just price.[22]

Lessio mentioned two cases in which a lower wage than the infimum is justifiable. The first involves the employer who hires a worker without the need of his services and, responding to his supplications, hires him only out of mercy. Lessio informs the compassionate employer to feed the laborer, stating that he should compensate him only if his work and services are more highly valued than the nourishment he provides. The second case refers to those servants who want to work in order to learn how to do a job or to obtain a benefit.[23] As apprentices, they may justifiably receive below-minimum salaries.

Villalobos offered similar arguments. He declared that laborers can be paid in kind and cited the example of unproductive servants who produce enough for food and shelter only, or students who work for food and shelter only so long as the employer gives them time to study. He even mentioned people who pay to work in a place where they can learn special crafts.[24]

Joseph Gibalini defined the just wage as the one that takes into account the service of the employee, the abundance or scarcity of laborers in similar jobs and what is commonly paid in that specific place. He then repeated Molina's arguments, including one that might shock some twentieth-century moralists. He stated categorically that the employer need not take into account either the needs of the laborer or his family.[25]

---

[21] Ibid.

[22] Ibid.

[23] Ibid.

[24] Villalobos, *Summa,* p. 407.

[25] Joseph Gibalini, *De Usuris, Comerciis, Deque Aquitate & Usu Fori Lugdunensis* (Lyon, 1657), p. 27. The Latin text reads, *"Non egitur ad hanc aequitatem, suamque familiam sustentare; non enim tenetur herus dare quantum valent obsequia sibi praestanda attentis omnibus circumstantiis."*

Cardinal Juan de Lugo determined that a servant's salary is just if it is at least similar to the lowest salary (the infimum level) commonly paid in that place for that specific job. He advised that the high salaries that rich noblemen pay their servants need not be taken into consideration. In an argument similar to those of Molina, Lessio, Villalobos and others, Lugo declared that the just salary bears no relation to the needs of the laborer.

Together with Covarrubias, Silvestre, Molina and other Doctors, Lugo judged that the worker is not entitled to receive a salary when he is absent from his job due to sickness, except when the labor contract has a special clause explicitly establishing otherwise.[26] Some Late Scholastics mentioned other factors that influence wages, such as the cost of learning a craft or a profession. St. Bernardino noted that the longer the training and the apprenticeship period, the smaller the supply of workers to perform a specific job. Hence, the higher the salary to reward their services.[27] The Schoolmen acknowledged that, through changes in supply, costs also influence prices. The more "industry" is needed to produce a thing, *caeteris paribus,* the more esteemed it becomes. This is the reason why a lawyer or an architect earns more money than a ditch-digger. The former requires greater ability and a longer training period than the latter. The Scholastics applied the same reasoning to the costs of medicines in comparison to the costs of medicinal herbs.[28]

[26] Lugo, *De Iustitia et Iure* (Lyon, 1642), no. 57, quoted in Gibalini, *De Usuris,* p. 38.

[27] "Lawyers, medical doctors, diggers, wrestlers could all sell their labor at a higher price due to scarcity in the supply of their jobs." St. Bernardino of Siena, *Opera Omnia, De Evangelio Aeterno* (Venice, 1591), Sermon XXXV, art. 2, chaps. 2 and 3.

[28] Ibid.

Condemned Practices in the Labor Market

The Late Scholastics condemned unfair practices on the part of both employers and workers. A typical example is the payment of wages in kind when the contract establishes a cash wage.[29] St. Antonino stipulated that, if necessary, the contractor must sell his goods at a loss to pay the salary in the manner the contract requires.[30] The Doctors also decried the practice of using debased currency to pay wages that were contracted before the devaluation. De Roover notes that this was very common in St. Antonino's time.[31]

Scholastic reasoning denounces unfair worker practices as well. The Schoolmen criticized guilds and monopolies and qualified cabbaging as robbery.[32] Laborers who purposely damaged and spoiled their tools also suffered their censure. Noting that both employers and laborers are obligated to fulfill their contracts, Villalobos decreed that "the man who hired his labor for a daywage and did not work faithfully must restore his fault".[33]

With regard to the act of receiving a salary as reward for an immoral act, the Schoolmen condemned the immoral action itself, but not the salary. They stated that prostitutes, for example, sin by disobeying the Sixth Commandment, but not by receiving a price for their services.[34] The Schoolmen's attitude toward low-paid workers was not prompted by a lack of social consciousness. The consumer's and the laborer's welfare were a recurring topic in Late Scholastic economic discourse. Their condemnation of monopolies, frauds, force and high taxes are all directed toward the protection and benefit of the working people. Nonetheless, they never proposed the determination of a minimum wage sufficient to maintain the laborer and his

[29] It is important to note that contracts could be made in kind. At issue was not the just form of payment, but the fulfillment of the contract.

[30] Antonino, *Summa Theologica,* pt. II, titulo 1, chap. 17, no. 8, and pt. III, titulo 8, chap. 4, no. 4.

[31] Raymond De Roover, *Saint Bernardino,* p. 27.

[32] Ibid.

[33] Villalobos, *Summa,* p. 401.

[34] For a detailed discussion of this matter see pp. 137–138.

family. In the belief that fixing a wage above the common estimation level would only cause unemployment, they recommended other means.[35]

Reason allows us to distinguish between goals and means. One of the goals of the Schoolmen's economic policy recommendations, as of any other school of thought, is the betterment of the worker's condition. Nonetheless, they understood that tampering with the market would be inconsistent with their goals. These reasons, and not a lack of charity, were the basis of their proposals. Those who criticize Late-Scholastic wage-theory for a so-called "lack of compassion" demonstrate their lack of understanding of the market.

The protection of private property, the promotion of trade and the encouragement of commerce, the reduction of superfluous government spending and of taxes and a policy of sound money were all destined to improve the condition of the workers. They recommended private charity as a way to alleviate the sufferings of those who could not work. According to the Late-Scholastics, and in agreement with the Holy Scriptures, the rich are under obligation to help the poor. Money could be better used if the rich would reduce their superfluous spending and increase their alms. Among the solutions proposed by the Scholastics we can find recommendations to feed the poor instead of feeding dogs and to give to the needy instead of buying luxury goods. Other ways of helping the poor produced diverse reactions. Perhaps the biggest debate regarding this issue in mid-sixteenth-century Spain focused on the recommendations, by several Councils of the Church, to forbid foreign beggars. Domingo de Soto opposed such measures as they would violate the natural right to emmigrate. See for example *Deliberacion en La Causa de los Pobres.* People cannot be deprived the right to beg or to look for jobs in foreign countries.

---

[35] Domingo de Soto suggested lengthy solutions to the problems of poor people. *Deliberación en la Causa de los Pobres* (Madrid: Instituto de Estudios Políticos, 1965), p. 35.

10

PROFITS

As in the rest of their analyses, the Scholastics' major concern regarding business profit (and personal gain) was moral justification. Profits may arise from industrial activity or from trade. The Schoolmen were careful to note that production and negotiation alone do not justify profits. In keeping with their theory of value and prices, they concluded that profits are justified when they are obtained through buying and selling at just prices.

This body of opinion arose in the context of controversy. Noting that activities that can produce a monetary gain are subject to risk and uncertainty, Duns Scotus espoused a cost-of-production justification of profits. After proving the usefulness of merchants and businessmen, he recommended that the good prince take steps to assure merchants high-enough prices to cover both their costs and their risks.[1]

On the other hand, the great bulk of Late Scholastic authors employed powerful arguments to highlight the inconsistency and dangers inherent in cost-of-production profit theories. St. Bernardino of Siena concluded that it is legitimate for manufacturers and tradesmen to obtain a profit. He also said that it is impossible to establish the level of the just profit, noting, "If it is legal to lose it must be legal to win."[2] Citing the example of a merchant who bought a good in a province where its common and current price was 100 and then took the good to another province where the current, common price was 200 or 300, he declared that "you can legally sell at that price which is current in that community".[3] In the opposite case of buying at 100 and then finding that the common price has decreased to 50, St. Bernardino

---

[1] Duns Scotus, *Cuestiones sutilisima sobre las Sentencias* (Antwerp, 1620), p. 509.

[2] St. Bernardino of Siena, *Opera Omnia* (Venice, 1591), bk. IV, Sermon XXX, p. 135.

[3] *"Tu potes licet vendere pro illo pretio, pro quo communiter currit."* Ibid.

recognized that it was natural for the merchant to lose. It is the nature of business that sometimes you win and sometimes you lose, depending on price variations.[4]

Saravia de la Calle stated categorically that entrepreneurial activity and trading are, by definition, subject to profit and loss and that such profits and losses should depend on the evolution of prices. When there is a great abundance of goods and merchandise, it is probable that prices will drop, and many merchants will suffer a loss. As Saravia noted, "in this case it is just that they lose, because otherwise we would never find a case where merchants justly lose; they would always win".[5] He explained that when changes in prices produce a profit, it is a just profit, and the same is true of losses.[6] Therefore,

> those who measure the just price by the labour, costs, and risk incurred by the person who deals in the merchandise or produces it, or by the cost of transport, or the expense of travelling to and from the fair, or by what he has to pay the factors for their industry, risk and labour are greatly in error, *and still more so are those who allow a certain profit of a fifth or tenth.* For the just price arises from the abundance or scarcity of goods, merchants and money, as has been said, and not from costs, labour and risk. *If we had to consider labour and risk in order to asses the just price, no merchants would ever suffer a loss, nor would abundance or scarcity of goods and money enter into the question.*[7]

Juan de Medina was one of the most articulate critics of the idea that merchants should always be able to sell at a profit. He argued that when the price of their commodities rises, sellers sometimes make a big profit, even when they incurred "little or no spending at all". When prices go down, the merchant should therefore feel the loss, "although he made large expenditures".[8] It would be unjust for the

[4] Ibid.

[5] Luis Saravia de la Calle, *Tratado muy provechoso de Mercaderes* (Madrid, 1949), p. 51.

[6] Ibid.

[7] Ibid., p. 50. Quoted in Marjorie Grice-Hutchinson, *The School of Salamanca* (Oxford, Clarendon Press, 1952), p. 48.

[8] Juan de Medina, *De Contractibus* (Salamanca, 1550), q. XXXVIII, p. 109.

merchants not to be held responsible for their losses to the same extent that they are entitled to their profits:

> Those who by their own will go into business . . . must expose themselves to profit and loss. And when they suffer a loss they must not transfer it to the buyers [consumers] or to the republic.[9]

The only circumstance in which Medina stated that the businessman should be protected against loss is in the case of government-fixed prices. When the merchant consummates a trade in obedience to a king's mandate, the just king will see to it that his costs are covered and his obedience rewarded.[10] It was clear for Medina that the practice of subsidizing losses harms not only the consumers, but also society as a whole (the republic). Mariana concurred:

> Those who, for seeing the demise of their business, cling to the magistrates [authority] as a shipwrecked person to a rock and attempt to alleviate their difficulties at the cost of the state are the most pernicious of men. All of them must be rejected and avoided with extreme care.[11]

García criticized merchants and businessmen who avow that they always have the right to earn a profit:

> This is a very big mistake and a diabolic persuasion because the art of business and of those who make money buying and selling must be equally open to profits and losses, depending on *luck* [fortune].

Since the merchant may realize legitimate gain when, "by *chance,* one can sell clothes at a higher price than their cost", García concluded

---

[9] "*Qui enim propria voluntate negotiationes huiusmodi suscipit, utrique pariter se debet exponere, lucro, scilicet, & dano. Quod si aliquando damnum sentiat, non emptoribus, aut reipub., sed sibi imputandum.*" Ibid.

[10] See p. 100.

[11] Juan de Mariana, *Del Rey y de la Institución Real,* in *Biblioteca de Autores Españoles,* Rivadeneyra, vol. 31 (Madrid: Editions Atlas, 1950), p. 532.

that it is unreasonable to follow a different rule when luck is against the merchant.[12]

With regard to the question of luck, the Late Scholastics even endorsed profit through gambling. Soto specified that such activity constitutes a voluntary exchange:

> No one can doubt that by natural law one can through a game transfer his property to another; because as has been said, the exchange of property that is more in agreement with nature is the one that is done according to the owner's free will.[13]

He emphasized that such voluntary exchange is a sort of contract. Those who would condemn such a contract on the basis of its uncertain outcome are mistaken "because many licit human businesses are trusted to the uncertainties of fortune".[14] Soto judged that the players do not sin if they desire to obtain a profit with their game, or if they play for the desire and love of profits.[15] Profits, by themselves, are morally indifferent. They can be used in a good or an evil manner, for a good or for a bad purpose.[16] According to St. Thomas, profits are an appropriate immediate goal for business (*negotiationis finis*).[17]

---

[12] Francisco García, *Tratado Utilisimo de Todos los Contratos, Quantos en los Negocios Humanos se Pueden Ofrecer* (Valencia, 1583), p. 251.

[13] Domingo de Soto, *De Iustitia et Iure* (Madrid: IEP, 1968), bk. IV, qu. V, art. 2, fol. 111–12.

[14] Ibid.

[15] Ibid. According to this author, he who ardently desires profits does not commit a *mortal* sin as long as he employs neither violence nor fraud. In this context, the Scholastics reminded their readers that to pursue an ultimate end other than God is to break the First Commandment.

[16] According to St. Thomas Aquinas, "Profit . . . while it may not carry the notion of anything right or necessary, does not carry the notion of anything vicious or contrary to virtue either. There is, therefore, nothing to stop profit being subordinated to an activity that is necessary, or even right. And this is the way in which commerce can become justifiable." The text in Latin reads: *"Lucrum . . . etsi in sui ratione non importet aliquid honestum vel necessarium, nihil tamen importat in sui ratione vitiosum vel virtuti contrarium. Unde nihil prohibet lucrum ordinari ad aliquem finem necessarium vel etiam honestum. Et sic negotiatio licita reddetur."* *Summa Theologica* (London: Blackfriars, 1975), II–II, qu. 77, art. 4, reply.

[17] Ibid.

St. Antonino phrased it:

> As every agent acts to attain an end, the man who works in agriculture, in wool, in industrial and other similar activities, the immediate end he pursues is gain and profit.[18]

Among the motives that justify profits, St. Thomas mentioned the following:

1. To provide for the businessman's household.
2. To help the poor.
3. To ensure that the country does not run short of essential supplies.
4. To compensate the businessman's work.
5. To improve the merchandise.[19]

He also ascribed legitimacy to profits obtained from price variations in response to local changes as well as those earned through the lapse of time. Furthermore, he allowed for profits that would compensate the risks of transport and delivery.[20]

To say that profits are a legitimate *immediate* end for those who engage in business does not contradict the Schoolmen's condemnation of those who pursued profits as their *ultimate* end. One of the most colorful issues they explored in this regard is the question of whether a prostitute is entitled to keep the profits she obtained by selling her body. Their answer was very cautious. Although as moralists they condemned the act of prostitution, they stated that such women have the right to receive monetary compensation for their services. This attitude toward immoral acts is simply the effect of putting into practice the Thomist principle that not every prohibition or recommendation of normative natural law needs a positive law to enforce it. As Father F. C. Copleston remarked,

---

[18] Sant' Antonino of Florence, *Summa Theologica,* in Raymond De Roover, *Saint Bernardino* (Cambridge, Mass.: Kress Library, 1967), pp. 14–15. Pedro de Aragón also wrote that "profit is the end of business" (*Lucrum est negotiationis finis*). *De Iustitia et Iure* (Lyon, 1596), p. 455.

[19] Aquinas, *Summa,* II–II, qu. 77, art. 4, reply.

[20] Ibid. The Schoolmen repeated these concepts with considerable accuracy.

It does not follow [in St. Thomas' philosophy] that every precept and prohibition of the natural moral law should be embodied in legislation; for there may be cases in which this would not conduce to the public good.[21]

St. Antonino noted that many sinful contracts (such as prostitution) are permitted for the utility of the republic, although this does not mean that they themselves are good.[22]

Some decades later, Conradus Summenhart wrote in his *De Contractibus* that prostitutes "who, by agreement, receive a price, sin by prostituting themselves, but they do not sin by receiving payment".[23] Martín de Azpilcueta concurred:

> Prostitutes, who earn a profit with their ill-fated bodies, although they sin in that, do not sin in taking their salary and they are not obliged to pay it back, and moreover, they can even claim what was promised to them.[24]

Antonio de Escobar was one of the first authors to generalize the Doctors' conclusions regarding prostitution and apply them to other profitable activities. He deduced that, although the sale of a prostitute's favors was evil, it caused pleasure, and things that cause pleasure merit a price. Furthermore, the prostitute's fee is freely rendered (no one can say that a man was obliged to go to a brothel). Noting that most other Scholastic authors shared this conclusion, Escobar stipulated that we must reason in the same way when analyzing other types of profit: no one can be obliged to make restitution of profits that were

---

[21] Frederick Copleston, *Thomas Aquinas* (London: Search Press, 1976), p. 240. St. Thomas Aquinas wrote that human law rightly allows some vices, by not repressing them. It should only forbid those vices which would render human society impossible: "thus human law prohibits murder, theft and such like". *Summa,* I–II, qu. 96, art. 2.

[22] St. Antonino of Florence, *Repertorium totius summe auree domini Antonini Archipresulis florentini ordinis predicatoris* [*Summa Theologica*] (Lyon: Johannes Cleyn, 1516), Pt. III, titulo VI, chap. III.

[23] Conradus Summenhart, *De Contractibus* (Venice, 1580), trat. I, q. VII.

[24] Martín de Azpilcueta, *Manual de Confesores y Penitentes* (Salamanca, 1556), pp. 198–199.

obtained without fraud, lies or extortion.[25] Quoting St. Augustine, Pedro de Aragón specified, "it is not business, but businessmen who are evil".[26]

[25] "*Non debet restituere quia licet actus ille non sit vendibilis, cum non sit licite ponibilis, non est tamen contra iustitiam eius venditio, qua enim parte delectabilis est, dignus est pretio. Et quia dans meretrici mere libera donat. . . . Haec sententia communis quidem vera omnino est. Moneo tamen, hoc intelligendum de lucro, quod non per fraudem et mendacia ab amasio sit extortum.*" Antonio de Escobar y Mendoza, *Universae Theologiae Moralis* (Lyon, 1662), D. XXXVII.

[26] "*Vitia sunt negotiantis non negotii. Negotium, inquit Augustinus, non facit me malum, sed mea iniquitatis.*" Pedro de Aragón, *De Iustitia et Iure* (Lyon, 1596), p. 458.

11

INTEREST AND BANKING

The Condemnation of Interest

Several excellent modern treatises analyze the Scholastic authors' opposition to loan interest.[1] In this, as in most other major issues, the Doctors espoused Thomist arguments, declaring

1. That money by itself is sterile.
2. That interest is a price charged by the lender for the use of money that already belongs to the borrower.
3. That interest is a price charged for time, a possession common to all.

Aristotle introduced the concept of money as valueless in itself. St. Thomas and his Late-Scholastic followers agreed with Aristotle's teachings, as did the Canonists. Diego Covarrubias y Leiva stressed that

> money brings forth no fruit from itself nor gives birth to anything. On this account it is inadmissible and unfair to take anything over and above the sum loaned for the use of that sum. . . . This would be not so much taken from money, which brings forth no fruit, as from the industry of another.[2]

---

[1] Bernard W. Dempsey, *Interest and Usury* (Washington, D.C.: American Council on Public Affairs, 1943); T. F. Divine, *Interest: An Historical and Analytical Study in Economics and Modern Ethics* (Milwaukee, Wis.: Marquette University Press, 1959); Benjamin N. Nelson, *The Idea of Usury* (Princeton: Princeton University Press, 1949), J. T. Noonan, *The Scholastic Analysis of Usury* (Cambridge, Mass.: Harvard University Press, 1957); J. A. Schumpeter, *History of Economic Analysis* (New York: Oxford University Press, 1954), pp. 101–107.

[2] Diego Covarrubias y Leiva, *Variarum resolutionum,* III, chap. 1, no. 5., quoted in E. Böhm-Bawerk, *Capital and Interest* (South Holland, Ill.: Libertarian Press, 1959), p. 14.

The second argument defines interest as a price paid for the use of money. The Scholastics noted that due to the nature of money, it is consumed in the act of being used. As is true of any other perishable or generic good (e.g., bread or wine), the use of money is therefore inseparable from its substance. A house, on the other hand, can be rented and remain useable after termination of the rental contract. Its use is therefore distinct from its consumption. According to this theory, renting money or charging for its use constitutes charging for something that does not exist.

The third argument invalidates interest by defining it as the sale of time, which is not private property. It first appeared in a small book entitled *De Usuris* and commonly attributed to St. Thomas Aquinas. If this authorship has been correctly assigned, St. Thomas came very close to discovering the essence of interest rates (i.e., time preference). Due to his belief that no one should charge for the use of time, he did not pursue this line of thought.[3]

St. Bernardino, nonetheless, pointed out that in certain cases time could be sold.[4] He distinguished two aspects of time: as duration *per se*[5] and as duration applicable to a certain good. The latter would allow the good to be used for a certain job. St. Bernardino concluded that, in this sense, time could be regarded as private property and therefore sold.[6]

On the other hand, the Scholastic authors agreed with Roman lawyers that the extrinsic titles *damnum emergens, lucrum cessans* and *poena conventionalis* could justify an interest payment to a lender. *Damnun emergens* provides that the lender is entitled to ask the borrower for compensation whenever he incurs losses due to the loan. Accord-

---

[3] Böhm-Bawerk discusses this topic in *Capital and Interest.*

[4] *"Tempus proprium venditoris ab eo licite potest vendi, quando temporalem utilitatem temporali pretio apretiabilem in se includit."* St. Bernardino of Siena, *Opera Omnia* (Venice, 1591), Sermon XXXIV, *De Temporis Venditione,* p. 322.

[5] *"Quaedam duratio, et hoc modo tempus est quid commune omnium, & nullo modo vendi post."* Ibid.

[6] *"Quaedam duratio applicabilis alicui rei, quae duratio, atque usus est alicui concensus ad eius opera excercenda: & hoc modo tempus est proprium alicuius . . . & huiusmodi tempus licite vendi potest."* Ibid.

ing to *lucrum cessans,* the lender may ask the borrower to compensate him for the gain he forgoes by not investing his money elsewhere.[7] *Poena conventionalis* imposes a penalty on tardy repayment.

The concomitant endorsement of Roman acceptance of interest rates and Thomist interdictions against them led to long and complicated discourse. As Schumpeter noted in *History of Economic Analysis,* the "Scholastic Doctors did not much more agree on the theory of interest than do we."[8] Nonetheless, he asserted that they "launched the theory of interest".[9]

In 1637, Fray Felipe de la Cruz published a book dedicated exclusively to the problem of interest.[10] Of all the Scholastic authors, he demonstrated the most liberal attitude toward interest rates. He began his discussion with the example of a gentleman who asked a nobleman to lend him four thousand silver ducats, promising to return the principal in the same silver money together with 12 percent interest for every year he did not return the principal. On the maturity date he returned the 4,000 ducats and nothing more, saying that to pay any amount above this would be usurious.

Attacking the hypothetical borrowers' reasoning, De la Cruz declared that it is licit to garner profit for justice and through gratitude. St. Thomas Aquinas had acknowledged the same point:

> The other ground for making compensation for a benefit received is the obligation of friendship, and here what really counts is the spirit in which the benefit is conferred rather than its quantity. But a legal obligation is hardly an appropriate sanction for such a debt, since it introduces a note of necessity that tends to stifle any spontaneous return.[11] . . . A person is, however, entitled to accept, and even to ask

---

[7] This second extrinsic title was subject to limitations. According to the preceding definition, an acceptance of *lucrum cessans* would have jeopardized their condemnation of interest. The Late Scholastics permitted it between merchants only.

[8] Schumpeter, *History of Economic Analysis,* p. 104.

[9] Ibid., p. 101.

[10] Felipe de la Cruz, *Tratado Unico de Intereses* (n.p., 1637). For complete title reference, see p. 24, above.

[11] St. Thomas Aquinas, *Summa Theologica* (London: Blackfriars, 1975), II–II, qu. 78, art. 2, reply obj. 2.

for and to expect, some service or the expression of some sentiment, provided it is motivated by good will and not by a feeling of obligation, since good will cannot be measured in terms of money.[12]

No one can morally condemn a person for giving a present to someone as a sign of gratitude. This is in agreement with natural and eternal law and is consistent with Scholastic justification of private property. St. Bernardino maintained that when one lends money without expecting a reward, "but the borrower liberally and spontaneously gives you something, for instance, a 10 percent profit, you can receive it".[13] Vitoria conceded that if the lender receives compensation (without having signed a contract or making any implicit agreement), there is nothing wrong with the contract because it is legal to receive donations. Furthermore, no one can be required to worsen his own condition by granting a loan. Saravia de la Calle admitted that in cases where the motives for paying interest can be qualified as benevolence, it is legitimate.

> There can be good intentions on the part of those who lend money and those who receive it. In this way, both the one who receives and the one who gives do so for benevolence and not by obligation. In these cases there is no usury or restitution.[14]

Molina, Rebelo, Bonacina and Salón made the point that gratitude may be expressed monetarily.[15] St. Antonino and Lessio carried the point further, maintaining that the lender is empowered to impose a civil obligation to reward the lender's largesse.[16] For La Cruz, it was completely logical for a civil code to compel people to do something that they are already obliged to do by natural and eternal law ("which

---

[12] Ibid., reply obj. 3.

[13] *"Si sua sponte, et liberalitate tibi dat aliquid, vel decem pro centenario de lucro tu potes accipere."* Bernardino (Venice, 1591), *Opera Omnia,* bk. 4, Sermon XXX, p. 138.

[14] Luis Saravia de la Calle, *Tratado muy Provechoso,* p. 78.

[15] La Cruz, *Tratado Unico,* p. 1.

[16] According to Antonino of Florence, merchants were not obliged to charge the same price for goods sold on credit as for goods sold for cash. Quoted in La Cruz, *Tratado Unico,* p. 2. See also Leonardo Lessio, *De Iustitia et Iure* (Antwerp, 1626), bk. 2, chap. 20, 3–19.

praises gratitude and abhors ingratitude".)[17] In support of the propriety of compensation, he quoted Bañez as saying that it is not sinful to expect a profit based on gratitude.[18] La Cruz then reported that Fray Luis de San Juan had declared that one can make a loan with the primary or secondary intention of receiving a monetary sign of gratitude. If the borrower can freely make a written promise to pay a sum above the principal, then the lender does not sin in demanding that such payment be made. In this regard, he quoted Pedro de Ledesma, noting that free-will in both parties (lender and borrower) is as much of a condition for a just exchange in borrowing as it is in the exchange of other economic goods.[19]

Furthermore, La Cruz acknowledged that such contracts can be favorable to the republic, and it is therefore contrary to the common good to outlaw them.

> A doctrine that comes from St. Thomas, and is well praised by Gerson, is that all contracts that are tolerated by and are fruitful to the republic must not be easily condemned.[20]

He argued that when the lender undertook not to request repayment of the principal for a notably long time (perhaps even a lifetime), he could expect monetary compensation. Said payment would reward his expansiveness with regard to the due date. As such, it would not constitute interest. The Scholastics did not consider this to be an interest payment. The lender does not charge a price for the loan, but rather for the obligation. "And as St. Thomas' disciples teach, this obligation can be esteemed with a price."[21] La Cruz then established that the problem is not a matter of rate (i.e., 5 or 10 percent), but of principle. The rate "cannot be given as something fixed or determined,

---

[17] La Cruz, *Tratado Unico,* p. 2.

[18] The Latin text reads: *"Intendere lucrum, sive principali intentione, sive minus principali, sive primaria, sive secundaria, non ex obligatione civili, sed ex gratitudine, nullum est omnino peccatum."* Domingo de Bañez, *De Iustitia et Iure Decisiones* (Salamanca, 1594), qu. 78, s.v. "usura" fol. 586, in La Cruz, *Tratado Unico,* p. 4.

[19] La Cruz, pp. 2, 4.

[20] Ibid., p. 7.

[21] Ibid.

because it can be increased according to the sum one gives and lends".[22] This applies to the prices of other goods as well. The market does not offer one single price, but rather an infimum price (the cheap price), a medium one and a rigorous (or expensive) one. "And the same good can be sold for 8, 10 or 12 and they can all be just prices."

Aristotle's dictum *"Pecunia non parit pecuniam"* (money does not beget money) constitutes a resounding rejection of interest rates. Felipe de la Cruz criticized this generalization, saying that by itself, money is fruitless, but it renders fruit when assisted by industrious human action, especially in commerce and trade. If people realize that, then

> I do not know how they can say this [Pecunia . . .] unless they all want to be deaf to the voice of reason, because experience in contracts teaches what I am saying. And it is known that when aided by human industry, money multiplies itself. Although this is the main cause of the profitability of money, it is not the only one. Money is partially responsible because of its qualities. . . . Plants and trees are also less fruitful if they are not aided [by human action].[23]

Since present money is worth more than a claim on future money, La Cruz did not condemn the common practice of charging interest. Disclosing that the kingdom of Valencia enjoyed Papal permission to charge 10, 12 and even 13 percent interest (depending on the circumstances), he declared that if cities and guilds are permitted to behave in this way, the citizens should also be allowed to do so.[24] He then described the case of a man who saved money and then lost the ability to earn more money through his own work. La Cruz believed

[22] Ibid., p. 8. Fray Luis de Alcalá reported that twenty-two Scholastic Doctors were in favor of considering the loans granted by a person who can earn money with his savings to be loans of a productive good. In this case, the lender may justly charge a percentage a little lower than his expected profit. He should deduct a percentage for the risk he will have to run to obtain that expected profit. It is important to remember that for Alcalá (as for many other authors) there is no certainty of profits, so a lender may not charge a lending rate equal to his expected profit.

[23] Ibid., pp. 11–12.

[24] Ibid., p. 13.

that it would be more natural for this man to lend his money out to earn interest than to consume his capital little by little. Addressing those who endorse a 5 percent interest rate, he insisted that they cannot then condemn a rate of 10 percent, because it is a matter of principle and not of amount. La Cruz elaborated important reasons why a merchant can sell at a higher price in the future than in the present. He stated categorically that "the right to receive money in the future has less value than money received in the present". In this regard, he quoted Saa and Navarro, who noted that by

> using the money [the owner] can obtain many benefits, as he can make contracts to increase his profits . . . and he can also solve some unexpected problems (such as sickness, fines or any other unanticipated circumstance). It can happen that problems arise and he will be left without the money that has been lent. Doesn't all this suffering due to privation deserve a reward, and doesn't it have some value?[25]

Remarking that the reward should depend on the amount of money and the period of time for the loan, he quoted Toledo: "the money that is absent has less value than present money".[26]

Despite Schumpeter's praises of Late-Scholastic interest analysis, it is safer to conclude with De Roover:

> The usury doctrine was the Achilles heel of scholastic economics. It involved the schoolmen and their sixteenth-century and seventeenth-century successors in insuperable difficulties that contributed greatly to bringing their whole doctrine into disrepute.[27]

Banking

Molina's analysis of banking is of utmost interest, for he surmised that bankers are the real owners of the money they handle. When they

[25] Ibid.

[26] Ibid., p. 10, Toledo (bk. 5, chap. 54, n. 2).

[27] *International Encyclopedia of the Social Sciences* (New York: Free Press, 1968), s.v. "Economic Thought, Ancient and Medieval Thought" by Raymond De Roover.

receive a deposit they do not promise to return the same money, but rather an equal sum of money. Their only legal obligation is to have the sum ready when their clients demand it.[28] *Legally,* if a banker cannot fulfill his obligations (because he has invested a more than reasonable part of the deposits in other dealings), he must not only repay all the money but also add a sum to compensate for the damage he has caused the depositor by not paying him on time. *Morally* he sins by endangering his own capacity to meet his debts, even if in the long run he suffers no legal difficulties because his speculations with the client's funds turned out well.[29]

Since Molina also justified the discounting of documents and many other banking operations, we may conclude with Fransisco Belda that he "approves one by one nearly all the possibilities of credit creation".[30] Soto was among the first Scholastic writers to describe and approve credit creation on the part of banks. It is customary, he remarked,

> that if a merchant deposits cash with a bank, the bank will guarantee to repay a larger sum. If I deposit 10,000 with the banker, he will repay me 12,000 or perhaps 15,000, because it is very profitable for a banker to have cash available. There is no evil in this.[31]

The Schoolmen also addressed the issue of whether it is good or bad to discount bills (i.e., to buy documents or letters of exchange at a price lower than their nominal value). Their opinion was unanimous: whenever one could claim the existence of one of the usual circumstances (*lucrum cessans, damnum emergens, periculum sortis*), the discounting of bills could not be condemned. They disagreed, however, in regard to other discounting circumstances. Cajetan and Azpilcueta justified discounts in all cases.[32] Citing Panormitano, Belarmino and Parra,

---

[28] Molina, *De Iustitia et Iure* (Moguntiae, 1614), bk. 2, disp. 408, nn. 1–7.

[29] Francisco Belda, "Etica de la Creacion de Créditos según la Doctrina de Molina, Lesio, y Lugo", *Pensamiento* 19 (1963): 62.

[30] Ibid., p. 70. Cardinal Juan de Lugo's approach is similar.

[31] Domingo de Soto, *De Iustitia et Iure* (Madrid: IEP, 1968), bk. 6, qu. II, art. 1, quoted in Marjorie Grice-Hutchinson, *Early Economic Thought in Spain, 1177–1740* (London: Allen & Unwin, 1975), p. 104.

[32] Belda, "Etica", p. 70.

Lessio determined that we should treat the sale of a document like the sale of any other good, with its price determined by common estimation, supply and demand. He concluded that the right to money in the future (money absent) should therefore be esteemed less than money in the present.[33] As Vitoria acknowledged, the phrase "have one" has more value than "I will give you two".[34] Cajetan was one of the most "liberal" authors in this regard. After specifying that the sale of a debt is similar to any other sale, he added that no one is willing to pay a sum of money in the present for the "right to the same amount of money in the future".[35] Cajetan concluded that the right to something in the future is barren until its maturity date. For that reason, prices will vary. This is what happens with the price of a plot of land that cannot be put into immediate production in comparison to one that can or with green fruit as opposed to ripe produce. Many Jesuit authors criticized this analysis, noting that, taken to its ultimate consequences, it would justify interest rates.[36]

The opponents of this position made the point that if such discounts were authorized, it would be very easy to disguise usurious contracts. One can agree with their analytical conclusion and disagree with their moral condemnation.

Since in the sixteenth century it was nearly impossible to issue a bill of exchange without incurring any risk and without foregoing the possibility of profits (*lucrum cessans*), justification of these actions became commonplace. Lessio was very lenient in his criticism of the custom (in Antwerp) of fixing the rate that a borrower had to pay for "depriving" the lender of his money at 6 to 12 percent. Molina added that it is proper to receive recompense for granting a guarantee (or pledge) for a loan to a friend. Cajetan, Soto, Conradus Summenhart,

---

[33] Lessio, *De Iustitia,* bk. 2, chap. 21, dub. 8, nn 66–71.

[34] *"Plus valet hoc tribuo; quam tribuenda duo; mas vale un toma, que dos te daré."* Francisco de Vitoria, *Opera Omnia* (Salamanca, 1934), bk. IV, p. 170.

[35] Cajetan, *Commentarium in Summam Theologicam S. Thomae* (Lyon, 1568), qu. 77, pp. 268–271.

[36] Lessio, bk. 2, chap. 23, dub. 1, p. 315.

Navarro and Covarrubias all concurred. The service rendered by the man who guarantees a loan with his money has a price that can be established by common estimation. It is an expensive service, and this is the reason why the guarantor may justifiably receive a reward. The basic cost is the added responsibility of the guarantor.[37]

Many of the Late Scholastics (Molina, Conradus Summenhart, Cajetan, Soto, Navarro and Medina) also decreed that the business-man who deals in currency exchange may charge a price for his services, but not for the time factor. They understood that future money has a lower value than present money, but for them, the underlying cause was not mere passage of time. As Belda correctly points out, this does not mean that Molina minimized the significance of the time element in economic dealings.[38]

The Doctors' conclusion was that when, due to the passage of time, the lender ceases to obtain a profit (*lucrum cessans*), then he may request compensation. Molina cited a case involving a clear analysis of how certain interest restrictions would produce a situation where everyone (the decent money dealers, the merchants and society as a whole), with the exception of the unscrupulous money dealers, would be worse off.[39] Molina posed the question of whether a person who advances money for a village fair may charge a fee in proportion to the time between the moment when he advanced the money and the moment when the fair takes place. If this is not allowed, the business-men who deal with money will not be prepared to lend it. Since commissions vary in proportion to the supply of money (and the demand for it), the rate will rise, and everyone will suffer. Only dishonest businessmen will profit from this situation. Molina rea-soned that the need for these exchanges should determine the commis-

---

[37] Belda, "Etica", p. 59.
[38] Ibid.
[39] Molina, *De Iustitia,* bk. 2, d. 404, n. 6.

sion: the greater the need, the higher the rate.[40] Azpilcueta also proffered an interesting point of view:

> Nor is it true that to use money, changing it at a profit, is against nature. Although that is not the first and principal use for which money was invented, it is nonetheless an important secondary use. To deal in shoes for a profit is not the chief use for which they were invented, which was to protect our feet; but that does not mean that to trade shoes is against nature.[41]

In the case of currency exchange, the Scholastics declared that the just price was the market price, determined by common estimation (demand and supply in an open market). T. F. Divine has argued that to take the market rate of interest as the criterion of the just price in an exchange of money available today for money available later is completely in accordance with Scholastic thought. Only in this way, he concludes, will there be "mutual advantage to buyer and seller, which Aristotle and Aquinas clearly recognized".[42]

---

[40] Belda, "Etica", p. 60. Nearly two centuries after the beginning of the Salamanca school, the Jesuit Calatayud named Molina one of the most important classical Doctors and indicated that his approval of futures trading (involving interest discounts) was accepted as common doctrine. Father Calatayud, *Tratados y Doctrinas Practicas sobre Ventas y Compras de Lanas Merinas y Otros Generos y Sobre el Juego de Naypes, y Dados*... (n.p., 1758), p. 38.

[41] Martín de Azpilcueta, *Comentario resolutorio de usuras*, p. 58, quoted in Grice-Hutchinson, *Early Economic Thought*, p. 103.

[42] *New Catholic Encyclopedia*, vol. XIV, s.v. "Usury", by T. F. Divine.

PART THREE

LATE–SCHOLASTIC
ECONOMIC THOUGHT
A COMPARISON WITH
CLASSICAL LIBERAL DOCTRINES

12

LATE-SCHOLASTIC ECONOMICS IN COMPARISON WITH CLASSICAL LIBERAL ECONOMICS

Actions are the result of ideas. In studying the origin of ideas, we are actually studying the origin of actions. The ideas that gave birth to what has been called the free society were not the result of spontaneous generation. Adam Smith's *Wealth of Nations,*[1] for example, bears the imprint of earlier writings, and these were influenced by still earlier writings. The road by which ideas influence later thoughts and actions is not always straight and well marked. When an author makes specific quotations and acknowledgments of another writer, we may clearly recognize his influence. On the other hand, people often adopt the reasonings of authors unknown to them. Where there are great similarities between two different authors, we may conclude that one *might* have influenced the other. It is easy to see the road leading from some Late Medieval thought to Classical Liberal ideas. In other areas, the road is concealed.

There are interesting similarities and, in some cases, contradictions, between Late-Scholastic thought and the ideas of important members of the liberal school. Since the writings of Protestant authors such as Grotius and Pufendorf sometimes served as the conduit between Catholic Late-Scholastic thought and later writers, they must figure in any analysis of the influence of Scholastic thought.

The Physiocrats, the Classical Liberal authors and the "Austrian economists" form the core of Western free-market tradition. While acknowledging the considerable distance between the *laissez-faire* of the French economists and Austrians' theory, it is not inappropriate

---

[1] Adam Smith, *An Inquiry into the Nature and Causes of the Wealth of Nations, 1776,* edited by E. Cannan (New York: Modern Library, 1937).

to classify these three schools of thought as embracing the same ideal — the ideal of human freedom.

The following pages represent a part of the search for the uncertain origin of many modern ideas in the extensive field that the Late-Scholastic authors embraced. Several of the issues analyzed in the following paragraphs have been the central topic of extensive modern studies.[2] Nonetheless, there is room for new studies and more complete analyses.

Private Property

The Medieval Schoolmen declared that although private property was in agreement with natural law, it was not founded upon it. They found private ownership to be in accordance with such other natural rights as liberty and life. After explaining that natural law refers to self-evident principles, Domingo Bañez stated that private property was founded not on these, but on utilitarian principles ("the fields are not going to be sufficiently tilled").[3] It is interesting to note that while dealing with natural rights, Adam Smith developed a similar conclusion:

> The origin of natural rights is quite evident. That a person has a right to have his body free from injury and his liberty free from infringement unless there be a proper cause, nobody doubts. But acquired rights such as property require more explanation. Property and civil government very much depend on one another ... the state of property must always vary with the form of government.[4]

---

[2] Especially the Scholastic analysis of usury (see footnote 1 in Chapter 11), their theory of the just price (e.g., the works of Raymond De Roover, B. W. Dempsey and Marjorie Grice-Hutchison) and their political thought (e.g., Bernice Hamilton's *Political Thought in Sixteenth-Century Spain* [Oxford: Clarendon Press, 1963]).

[3] See pp. 53–54. Domingo de Soto also wrote in similar terms. *De Iustitia et Iure* (Madrid: IEP, 1968), bk. III, qu. 3, art. 1, English translation in Hamilton, *Political Thought in Sixteenth-Century Spain,* pp. 100–101.

[4] Adam Smith, *Lectures on Justice, Police, Revenue and Arms* (New York: Kelley & Millman, 1956), p. 8.

Smith explained that rights are either natural or acquired. Remarking that "the former need no explanation", he added that the right to property, however, is an acquired right and therefore requires discussion.[5] His argument is comparable to many Late Scholastic's conclusion that property is an *addition* to natural law and therefore falls under the jurisdiction of civil law. Ludwig von Mises, a staunch defender of the free society, also argued that the idea of private property was founded on utilitarian principles rather than natural law.[6]

Twentieth-century economists continue to use many of the arguments the Late Scholastics employed in defense of private property. Hans F. Sennholz pointed out that private ownership is a natural institution that facilitates orderly production and division of labor.[7] Von Wieser noted that property does not make sense in a world without scarcity.[8]

One of the favorite Late Scholastic arguments was that private property is one means for the achievement of a peaceful society. Many libertarians agree. Mises stated, "It is precisely in the defence of property that Law reveals most clearly its character of peacemaker".[9] Classical Liberal theory also parallels the Late Scholastic reasoning that private property allows a more productive economy. Mises pointed out that higher productivity results from the peace that a society that respects private property naturally enjoys.[10]

It is presently common for arguments against private property to

---

[5] Ibid., p. 107.

[6] "Private property is a human device." Ludwig von Mises, *Human Action* (New Haven, Conn.: Yale University Press, 1949), p. 679.

[7] Hans F. Sennholz, *Death and Taxes* (Washington, D.C.: Heritage Foundation, 1976), p. 12. William Graham Sumner wrote that "Private ownership of land is only division of labor", *What Social Classes Owe to Each Other* (New York: Harper & Row, 1883), pp. 50–51.

[8] F. von Wieser recognized that "the idea of the importance of property only originates in scarcity". "The Theory of Value: A Reply to Professor Macvane", *Annals of the American Academy of Political and Social Science* II (1891–1892): 600–628, reprinted in *Economic Thought,* edited by James A. Gherity (New York: Random House, 1969), p. 315.

[9] Ludwig von Mises, *Socialism,* (Indianapolis: Liberty Press, 1981), p. 34.

[10] Ibid.

begin with the premise of the "evil man". "As long as people don't mind exploiting their neighbors, we cannot have private property", they say. The Late Scholastics acknowledged the same unfortunate human trait. They also realized, however, that far from being a solution, common ownership would increase evil in society. Believing that "evil men will take more and add less to the barn of common goods", the Scholastics foresaw that evil men (thieves and misers, as Vitoria noted) would easily achieve the highest positions in such a society.

Current Roman Catholic doctrine endorses the natural right to private property.[11] It seems rather paradoxical that those who rejected the "natural right to property" now favor private ownership in a more consistent way than some who espouse it as a natural right.[12] The Scholastic treatment of property promotes an approach to the "social function" of private property that is very similar to the one many Classical Liberals shared. The Medieval Schoolmen favored private ownership because it allows property to be *used* in a more

[11] As Pope Leo XIII wrote in condemnation of the socialists, "In short, spurred on by greedy hankering after things present, which is *the root of all evils, which some coveting have erred from the faith* (1 Tim. vi. 10), *they attack the right of property, sanctioned by the law of nature,* and with signal depravity, while pretending to feel solicitous about the needs, and anxious to satisfy the requirements of all, they strain every effort to seize upon and hold in common all that has been individually acquired by title of lawful inheritance, through intellectual or manual labor, or economy in living." *The Great Encyclical Letters of Pope Leo XIII* (New York: Benziger Brothers, 1903), p. 23. [Italics mine.]

[12] The idea that proper use of private property must be compelled by law contradicts Pius XI's decree in *Quadragesimo Anno* (47): "In order to place definite limits on the controversies that have arisen over ownership and its inherent duties, there must be first laid down as a foundation a principle established by Leo XIII: The right of property is distinct from its use. That justice called commutative commands sacred respect for the division of possessions and forbids invasion of others' rights through the exceeding of the limits of one's own property; but the duty of owners to use their property only in a right way does not come under this type of justice, but under other virtues, obligations of which *cannot be enforced by legal action.* Therefore, they are in error who assert that ownership and its right use are limited by the same boundaries; and *it is much farther still from the truth to hold that a right to property is destroyed or lost by reason of abuse or non-use."* [Italics mine.]

beneficial manner. They believed that a private-property society will tend to be more peaceful, more productive and, over all, more moral.

Like the Schoolmen, Mises regarded ownership as the power to use economic goods. Stating that "an owner is he who disposes of an economic good",[13] he also recognized that, from a legal point of view, one can own a good even when it is not physically in his possession.[14] The Austrian economist differentiated ownership from the use of production factors. He found this to be particularly true in the case of production involving division of labor: "Here, in fact, the *having* is always two-fold: there is a physical *having* (direct), and a social *having* (indirect)".[15] Mises made the point that he who holds the commodity and uses it productively exercises *direct* ownership, while the "social *having* belongs to him who, unable to dispose physically or legally of the commodity, may yet dispose indirectly of the effects of its use".[16] His conclusion is that "natural ownership in a society which divides labour is shared between the producer and those for whose wants he produces".[17] Recognizing that in such a society *"no one is exclusive owner of the means of production"*,[18] Mises concludes that ownership is a social function.[19]

When protected by privileges (personal rights), ownership loses its social function. Late-Scholastic reasonings in favor of private property paved the way for the great nineteenth-century reformations. In every age—and the twentieth century is no exception—many have achieved possession through force and privilege. In the most recent decades of our age, there is therefore a tendency to interpret the social

---

[13] Mises, *Socialism,* p. 27.

[14] Ibid.

[15] Ibid., p. 30.

[16] Ibid.

[17] Ibid.

[18] Ibid., p. 31. [Italics mine.] Mises goes even further, remarking that "we should have to regard consumers as the true owners in the natural sense and describe those who are considered as the owners in the legal sense as administrators of other people's property". Ibid.

[19] Ibid., p. 680. Mises also cites the general interest as the reason for private property. Ibid., p. 454.

function of ownership differently. While retaining the term *private property,* many modern thinkers would preserve the institution in the formal sense only. According to them, "society" should determine how goods are to be used. "Liberation theology" and various collectivist schools of thought embrace the theory that not the chaffering of the market but, rather, force and law should dictate the social function of property. In this sense the Schoolmen's theory of private property's social function coincides much more with Mises' conclusions than with liberation theology.[20]

Private responsibility disappears in a society where owners may not decide how their goods will be used. When "society" directs the owner of a factory to invest in a certain field, to hire a certain number of workers at a prescribed salary and to sell his goods at a price fixed by authority, he cannot be held responsible if things go wrong. This theory dictates that "society" must assume the loss. It provides that the owner is still entitled to a "just profit". Profits and property thus lose their ties with consumer satisfaction. The paradoxical result is that, by attempting to use force to encourage the social function of ownership, government renders it impossible. In such a society, people struggle to accrue the favors of law rather than to satisfy the consumer. The struggle for power and the conflicts and clashes of interest groups thus supplant peaceful cooperation in the marketplace. Only in a free society is "ownership of the means of production not a privilege, but a social liability".[21]

---

[20] The most famous book in defense of liberation theology is *A Theology of Liberation* by Gustavo Gutiérrez (New York: Orbis Books, 1973). The following footnote appended to his text delineates his extreme stance: "A new man and a new society will not be possible unless labor comes to be understood as the only effective human principle, when the fundamental stimulus of the economic activity of man is social interest, when capital is subordinated to the work, *and the means of production come under social ownership.*" Ibid. [Italics mine.]

[21] Mises, *Human Action,* p. 308.

Public Finance

To believe in private property means to believe in limited government. The Late Scholastics decreed that government should be neither overpowerful nor above the people. Most aspects of human life were to be left free from state intervention.

The Doctors' avowal that people are above government, however, did not imply that they had confidence in the people's will or that they supported majority rule. They realized that majority support for a wrong idea or for an unjust policy could never guarantee that it was either *right* or *just*.

For the Schoolmen, the term "democracy" was not synonymous with "republic". They defined democracy as one of the systems that people may adopt in order to be governed. The rights people could enjoy in a given society were decidedly more important than the system—hence Mariana's remark that he had witnessed both effective republics and just monarchies.[22]

The objective of policy, according to the Medieval Doctors, is to favor the common good. This is in agreement with the principle that

[22] See p. 63. The Founding Fathers of the United States of America usually spoke of a republican and not of a democratic system. They understood the dangers of unlimited majority rule and of any other unlimited form of government as well. "The accumulation of all powers, legislative, executive, and judiciary, in the same hands, whether of one, a few, or many, and whether hereditary, self-appointed, or elective, may justly be pronounced the very definition of tyranny." *The Federalist Papers* no. 47. Late Scholastic ideas on government duties and the people's rights were very influential in Hispanic America. Two examples of this influence are Spanish priests' staunch defense of Indian rights (i.e., Bartolomé de las Casas, *Obras Escogidas* [Madrid: Ediciones Alas, 1957–58]) and the spreading of republican ideals through most of this region. Noted historians have argued that the ideas that guided the revolutionaries in some of the most important Spanish colonies in America were a result of Late-Scholastic teachings. Guillermo Furlong shared this opinion. He mentions Vitoria, Mariana, and Suarez as having great influence in Latin America. *Nacimiento y Desarrollo de la Filosofía en el Río de la Plata 1536–1810* (Buenos Aires: Ed. Kraft, 1952). Although this conclusion may be too strong, it is clear that the Late Scholastics cannot be regarded as defenders of the status quo or of a totalitarian form of government.

the general welfare is more important than individual interest.[23] In Late-Scholastic theory, the definition of the common good was not left to the whims of the king or of the popular majority. The Schoolmen knew that the clarification of policy goals and the selection of the proper means toward their attainment always involves a degree of arbitrariness. When the issue is should we have more policemen, fund a bigger army or build a new court house, there is no objective solution, no easy rule to follow.

Noting that policies to attain the common good should never run against the natural order and natural human rights,[24] the Late Scholastics defended American Indian rights to own property as well as to trade and to choose their own authorities. They realized, nonetheless, that individual interests will not always favor general well being. This notion of the common good is not extraneous to contemporary libertarian thought. Mises, for example, concluded that "the policy of Liberalism is the policy of the common good, the policy of subjecting particular interests to the public welfare".[25] The Schoolmen's idea of society, government and human rights is very similar to the one that believers in the free society endorse today. The Doctors' attitude toward government spending is closely related to their ideas on the nature of government and cannot be qualified as lenient. They condemned it, not only because they could understand the negative effects it would have on the economy, but also because it would mean infringement of property rights.

[23] Hispanic-Scholastic thought on this topic is analyzed by Hamilton in *Political Thought,* p. 57.

[24] After recognizing that each citizen is part of the community and that therefore the law laid down for them "must direct them toward the common good of the whole society, just as the parts of a body are in the service of the whole body," Soto stresses the ultimate good of the individual: "a member (that is, a part of a human body) has no existence distinct from the existence of the whole; nor is it capable in itself of right or injustice. But a man, although he is part of the community, is nonetheless a person existing for himself, and so capable of suffering injustice, which the state may not impose on him." *De Iustitia,* bk. IV, qu. 4, art. 1. Translation from Hamilton, *Political Thought,* pp. 30–31.

[25] Mises, *Socialism,* p. 456.

The Late-Scholastic rejection of inflation as a method of overcoming financial difficulties paved the way for their balanced-budget proposals. In their opinion, the monarch should endeavor to balance the budget by cutting spending, reducing subsidies and dismissing courtiers. One of the Schoolmen's primary concerns was the high level of taxation in their era. They rejected the financing of budget deficits through public debt. In their experience, not only did excessive borrowing by the state fail to reduce the burden of excessive spending, it also jeopardized the future of the kingdom.

For the Scholastics, the purpose of taxation was to raise the necessary revenue for just government. They declared that taxes should be moderate and proportional, making no reference whatsoever to taxation as a tool for equalizing wealth. The great majority of twentieth-century libertarians[26] also stated that taxes are the source of government revenue and not a tool for distributing wealth. They insisted that tax imposition should be enacted in accordance with the neutrality principle. A neutral tax is one that does not divert the operation of the market from the "natural" lines along which it would develop in the absence of taxation.[27] While acknowledging that it can never be achieved, Classical Liberals insist that neutral taxation should be the goal of fiscal authorities.[28]

In his claim for moderate taxes, Navarrete realized that excessive taxation could reduce the king's income (as few will be able to pay such high rates).[29] Some modern economists have recently argued in

---

[26] One branch of libertarians opposes all restrictions on private property and therefore rejects the idea of coercive appropriation of the goods of one group of people (i.e., government) on the part of another group, be it small or numerous. The intellectual leader of this group is Murray Rothbard, who espouses his ideas in such books as *Man, Economy and State: A Treatise on Economic Principles* (Princeton, N.J.: Van Nostrand, 1962); *Power and Market, Government and the Economy* (Menlo Park, Calif.: Institute for Humane Studies) and *For a New Liberty: The Libertarian Manifesto,* (New York: Collier Books, 1978).

[27] Mises, *Human Action,* p. 730.

[28] Ibid., p. 731.

[29] See p. 67.

similar terms, proposing tax reductions to increase tax revenue from the resultant higher level of production.

Mises was not far from this idea when he remarked that "every specific tax, as well as a nation's whole tax system, becomes self-defeating above a certain height of the rates."[30] In the field of economic ethics, the Late Scholastics were careful to point out that certain tax laws could oblige legally but not morally. They based this conclusion on their belief that an unjust positive law is not a true law, even though the government may have the power to enforce it.

The Theory of Money

Theories about the origin and nature of money directly influence discussion of the value of money and monetary policy recommendations. Those who avow that money is simply a legislative phenomenon are more prone to accept government interference in monetary issues. State intervention in the money market is commonly directed toward influencing the value of money.

Along with the Late Scholastics, Pufendorf, Adam Smith and the Austrians all explain the origin of money in an Aristotelian fashion. Pufendorf's writings bear the imprint of Late-Scholastic tradition. He explained that as societies developed, indirect exchange supplanted direct exchange:

> It was not easy for a man to secure such things as another would be willing to exchange for what he wanted, or which were equivalent to another's goods. And in civilized states where citizens are divided into different social orders, there must needs be several classes of men who cannot subsist at all, or else with the utmost difficulty, if this simple exchange of commodities and labour persists. It is per-

[30] Mises, *Human Action,* p. 734.

fectly plain that those nations that are unacquainted with the use of currency have no part in the advances of civilization.[31]

With regard to the factors that influence the value of money, Pufendorf lent greater importance to human interaction and consensus than to nature:

> But since this *function of money is not given it by any necessity arising from its nature, but by the imposition and agreement of men* . . . it is obvious that other materials can be and are used under stress of circumstances or by preference.[32] . . . But although the value of gold and silver, and of money, depends upon the imposition and agreement of men, the governors of states have not the freedom to change that value at their will, but must bear in mind certain considerations. . . . In the next place, money is created the better to aid commerce, not merely between citizens of the same state, but between those of different states. Therefore, if the sovereign of a state has set an outrageous value on his own coinage, he makes it of no use for the trade of his citizens with foreigners.[33]

Although the Physiocrat Turgot also explained the origin of money in an Aristotelian fashion,[34] he concluded that

> the constitution of gold and silver as money and universal money . . . [was achieved] without any arbitrary convention among men, without the intervention of any law, but *by the nature of things.*[35]

---

[31] Samuel Pufendorf, *De Jure Naturae et Gentium Libri Octo,* edited by J. B. Scott (London: Oceana, 1934), p. 690. He then quotes most of Aristotle's remarks concerning money, even that money helps commerce and commerce holds "the political communion together" (*Magna moralia* bk. I, chap. XXXIV [XXXIII]). Ibid., p. 691.

[32] Ibid., p. 692. Grotius, on the other hand, noted that money "acquires its function naturally", *De Jure Belli Ac Pacis Libri Tres,* edited by James Brown Scott (London: Oceana, 1964), bk. II, chap. XII, p. 354.

[33] Ibid., p. 693.

[34] "Everyone who has a surplus commodity, and has not at the moment any need of another commodity for use, will hasten to exchange it for money; with which he is more sure, than with anything else, to be able to procure the commodity he shall wish for at the moment he is in want of it." Anne Robert Jacques Turgot (New York: Macmillan, 1914) *Reflections on the Formation and the Distribution of Riches,* p. 39.

[35] Ibid.

According to Turgot, all money is essentially merchandise, and any commodity will serve for indirect exchanges.[36] The concept that "a purely conventional money is therefore an impossibility"[37] led to his decision that metals—especially gold and silver—were by nature the most appropriate goods to use as currency.[38]

Since Aristotle declared both convention and the nature of indirect exchange to be major factors influencing the origin of money, both Pufendorf's and Turgot's explanations could have developed from Aristotelian doctrines. Joseph Schumpeter labels these two arguments the Cartal and Metallist theories, respectively.[39] As did the Late Scholastics, Austrian economists developed their monetary theory upon Aristotelian foundations.[40] In accordance with a subjective theory of value, it is possible to conclude with Mises that "men have chosen the precious metals gold and silver for the money service on account of their mineralogical, physical and chemical features".[41] He further noted that the use of "gold—and not something else . . . as

[36] Ibid., p. 36.

[37] Ibid.

[38] "The metals, and especially gold and silver, are more fit for this purpose than any other substance. . . . All the metals, as one after the other they have been discovered, have been admitted into the exchanges in proportion to their real utility. . . . A piece of any metal, whatever it may be, has exactly the same qualities as another piece of the same metal, provided it is equally pure. . . . In expressing, then, the value of each commodity by the weight of the metal one gives in exchange we have the clearest, the most convenient, and the most exact expression of all the values; and henceforth it is impossible that it should not in practice be preferred to every other." Ibid., pp. 37–38.

[39] Joseph A. Schumpeter, *History of Economic Analysis* (New York: Oxford University Press, 1954), p. 63.

[40] Hans Sennholz wrote that "the only service rendered by money is that of medium of exchange. It cannot be consumed and cannot serve any productive end." *Age of Inflation,* p. 19.

[41] Mises, *Human Action,* p. 468.

money is merely a historical fact and as such cannot be conceived by catallactics".[42]

According to the Late Scholastics, the value of money should be determined in the same manner as the value of any other commodity.[43] They saw its utility and scarcity as the main factors influencing its value. Believing that the usefulness of money bore close relationship to its quantity, the Schoolmen noted that when money undergoes continuous debasements, people try to reduce their real cash holdings. A reduction in the legal value of money will therefore cause a price increase of similar proportions. They also remarked that the value of money is greatest where it is more urgently needed for transactions (e.g., at fairs).

The Late Scholastics in general — and Azpilcueta in particular — have been credited as the first formulators of the "quantity theory of money".[44] The quotations presented in Chapter 5 are sufficient proof that this credit is well deserved. The Medieval Schoolmen had knowledge of almost every factor influencing the value of money. They stated that, like any other good, it was subject to fluctuation. Nonetheless, money was expected to vary less in price than other goods. Turgot also recognized this natural variability in the "price" of

[42] Ibid. Catallactics is the science of exchanges in the market. "Its subject matter is all market phenomena with all their roots, ramifications, and consequences." Ibid., p. 234. Joseph A. Schumpeter classified Aristotelian monetary theory as belonging "to what Professor von Mises has described as 'catallactic' theories of money." *History of Economic Analysis,* p. 63.

[43] Turgot explained that the value of money is determined in the same way as the value of other commodities. *Reflections,* p. 42.

[44] Marjorie Grice-Hutchinson, *Early Economic Thought* in Spain, 1177–1740 (London: Allen & Unwin, 1975) p. 104. As Philip Cagan notes, "In one version of this theory — the quantity theory of money — the absolute level of prices is independently determined as the ratio of the quantity of money supplied to a given level of desired real cash balances. Individuals cannot change the nominal amount of money in circulation, but, according to the quantity theory of money, they can influence the real value of their cash balances by attempting to reduce or increase their balances. In this attempt they bid the prices of goods and services up or down, respectively, and thereby alter the real value of cash balances." Philip Cagan, "The Monetary Dynamics of Hyperinflation" in *Studies in the Quantity Theory of Money,* edited by Milton Friedman (Chicago: University of Chicago Press, 1956) p. 29.

money.[45] He acknowledged that a stable currency is a worthy goal, but perfect stability is not of this world.

Since Late Scholastics based their monetary-policy recommendations and analyses on their theory of the value of money, it is not surprising that, in the field of economic policy, they arrived at conclusions similar to those of modern libertarian authors. The Schoolmen avowed that currency debasement caused a revolution in fortunes, undermined political stability and violated property rights. It also created confusion in commerce (internal and foreign trade), leading to stagnation and poverty. Currency debasement, at least for Mariana, represented an instrument of tyrannical plunder.[46]

In the field of economic ethics, the Doctors condemned the use of currency debasement as a massive debt-liquidation process in real terms. Mariana severely criticized those princes who adulterated coinage standards to pay their debts. Other Late Scholastics specified that

[45] "This value is susceptible of change, and in fact does change continually; so that the same quantity of metal which corresponded to a certain quantity of such or such a commodity ceases to correspond to it, and more or less money is needed to represent the same commodity. When more is needed the commodity is said to be dearer, and when less is needed it is said to be cheaper; but one might just as well say that it is the money that is cheaper in the first case and dearer in the second. Not only do silver and gold vary in price as compared with all other commodities; but they vary in price among themselves according as they are more or less abundant." Turgot, *Reflections,* p. 41.

[46] Hans Sennholz includes similar arguments in his *Age of Inflation,* where he remarks that "when it covers its budgetary deficits [the government] with new money issues [the equivalent of currency debasements], it seizes real income and wealth from money holders. Its consumption is increased and that of the inflation victims reduced by a like amount, which explains the great popularity of inflation with monetary authorities, from Greek city tyrants to contemporary dictators and government officials." *Age of Inflation,* p. 19. We may compare this with Mariana's comment on p. 84 and p. 86 of this study. In another of his books Sennholz remarks that "inflation is sometimes described as a tax on the money holders. In reality, it is a terrible instrument for the redistribution of wealth." *Death and Taxes* (Washington, D.C.: Heritage Foundation, 1976), p. 48.

debts should be paid in the money that was current at the time of the contract.[47]

Samuel von Pufendorf employed similar arguments to criticize the policy of currency debasement.[48] He even mentioned Mariana (without citing his arguments). Pufendorf agreed that currency debasement would seriously undermine private estates. He declared that "if so much alloy is mixed with coins . . . the very coins themselves are forced to blush at their own baseness".[49] Pufendorf allowed that kings who resorted to this policy could be excused on the plea of necessity, "provided that the wrong is righted after the necessity has been removed".

Careful reading of Adam Smith's *Lectures* and his *Wealth of Nations* reveals that these arguments exercised influence on his thinking. He first noted the prevalence of monetary debasement in his *Lectures:*

> When for instance, on any important occasion, such as paying debts, or of soldiers, it [the government] has occasion for two millions, but has no more than one, it calls in the coin of the country, and, mixing with it a greater quantity of alloy, makes it come out two millions, as like as possible to what it was before. Many operations of this kind have been performed in every country.[50]

In *Wealth of Nations,* Smith repeated that "the raising of the denomination of the coin has been the most usual expedient by which a real public bankruptcy has been disguised under the appearance of a pretended payment".[51] The same volume contains Smith's severe censure of this practice.[52]

---

[47] After differentiating between the intrinsic and extrinsic value of money, Pufendorf stated that when the intrinsic value was modified (i.e., a change in the quantity or quality of the metal content of the coin), debts should be paid in the money that was current at the time of the loan. If the value of money changed due to the market, then the money in use at the maturity date should be accepted in payment. *De Jure Naturae,* p. 694.

[48] Ibid.

[49] Ibid.

[50] Smith, *Lectures,* p. 188.

[51] Smith, *Wealth of Nations,* p. 882.

[52] Ibid.

Trade

Stressing the importance of trade and commerce and noting that human society benefits from the exchange of goods, the followers of the Late Scholastics continued to offer elaborate proofs of the need for domestic and international trade. They discerned it as a need rooted in human limitations and geographical differences. Since distinct lands offered different products, the Schoolmen declared that only through commerce could any one country enjoy well-rounded and diversified provisions.[53]

Although Pufendorf recognized the benefits of commerce,[54] he was much more prone to advocate restrictions than the Hispanic Scholastics. His quotation from Libanius' *Orations,* iii, traces the origin of trade to Divine will:

> God has not bestowed His gifts upon every quarter, but has divided them according to regions, so as to incline men to social relations by the need of mutual assistance; and He has disclosed the avenues of trade, with the intent to bring to all mankind the common enjoyment of those things that are produced only among a few.[55]

Recounting that the ancient Athenians excluded the Megarians from all their markets and harbors, Pufendorf noted that the latter complained that this was contrary to the "common laws of justice". He did not concur fully with this complaint, commenting that "such an assertion allows many restrictions".[56] In Pufendorf's opinion, the state has the right to prevent foreigners from trading in those goods that are not absolutely necessary for existence, particularly "if our country thereby would lose a considerable profit or in some indirect way suffer any

---

[53] See pp. 90–91.

[54] "For a great advantage arises for all people from commerce, which makes compensation for the niggardliness, as it were, of the soil, which is not equally productive of everything, everywhere, and causes the product of one place only to appear to have a habitat in every land." Pufendorf, *De Jure Naturae,* pp. 368–369.

[55] Ibid., p. 369.

[56] Ibid.

harm".[57] In the context of the popularity of protectionist ideas in the seventeenth century, Pufendorf declined to censure the country that, to "favor the commonwealth", forbids the export of a certain good or regulates trade between nations. He therefore allowed the propriety of laws restricting imports "either because the state may suffer a loss from its importation, or that our own citizens may be incited to greater industry, and that our wealth may not pass into the hands of foreigners".[58] Quoting Plato in support of this opinion, he specifically criticized Vitoria's liberal attitude:

> For this reason the position of Franciscus a Victoria is certainly false when he maintains: "The law of nations allows every man to carry on trade in the provinces of others by importing merchandise which they lack and exporting gold and silver, as well as other merchandise, in which they abound."[59]

Noting that authority has the right to impose commerce restrictions for the same reason it has power to tax—for the good of the commonwealth—Pufendorf stipulated that the subjects may not exercise the same right.[60]

He specifically stated that "it would be inhuman and unjust to hinder a man, who wants to distribute among eager customers goods in which he abounds, from securing by exchange for his own use the necessities of which he stands in need."[61]

It was the Physiocrats who coined the phrase *laissez faire, laissez passer.* They adopted a favorable attitude toward commerce and trade. According to Turgot, the diversity of soils and the multiplicity of

[57] Ibid.
[58] Ibid., p. 370.
[59] Ibid.
[60] Ibid.
[61] Ibid., p. 371.

wants lead to the exchange of products.[62] He noted that commerce benefits human society, as "everyone profited by this arrangement, for each by devoting himself to a single kind of work succeeded much better in it".[63]

Adam Smith's conclusion that the division of labor causes the wealth of nations lends considerable support to the justification of domestic and international trade. Nonetheless, he was unable to divorce himself from the Mercantilist climate of opinion. The enemies of a commonwealth united by free trade frequently cite his advocacy of protective tariffs for the naval industry.[64]

Among the modern Classical Liberals, Ludwig von Mises regarded the division of labor and its counterpart (human cooperation) as the fundamental social phenomena.[65] He stated that the principle of the division of labor (and therefore of commerce) is founded on the laws of nature and is what makes human society possible:

> Human society is an intellectual and spiritual phenomenon. It is the outcome of a purposeful utilization of a universal law ... viz., the higher productivity of the division of labor. As with every instance of action, the recognition of the *laws of nature* is put into the service of man's efforts to improve his conditions.[66]

In Mises' opinion, not only does division of labor produce economic fruits, but also, within the framework of social cooperation, "there

---

[62] Turgot, *Reflections,* p. 3. "He whose land was only fit for grain and would produce neither cotton nor hemp would be without cloth wherewith to clothe himself. Another would have a piece of land fit for cotton which would not produce grain. A third would be without wood wherewith to warm himself. Experience would soon teach each what was the kind of product for which his land would be best adapted, and he would limit himself to the cultivation of that particular crop, in order to procure for himself the things he was devoid of by means of exchange with his neighbours; and these, having in their turn made the same reflections, would have cultivated the crop best suited to their field and abandoned the cultivation of all others." Ibid., p. 4.

[63] Ibid., p. 6.

[64] Smith, *Wealth of Nations,* pp. 429–430.

[65] Mises, *Human Action,* p. 157.

[66] Ibid., p. 145. [Italics mine.]

can emerge between members of society feelings of sympathy and friendship and a sense of belonging together".[67]

It cannot be said that Late Scholastic writings were free from Mercantilist beliefs.[68] Nonetheless, they favored freedom of commerce. Most of them were aware of the poverty that Spanish Mercantilist policies had caused in Hispanic America, since returning missionaries belonging to various religious orders described these inconveniences in great detail. A free and united commonwealth was not far from their Catholic perspective.

Value and Price

The Late-Scholastic theory of value and price shaped subsequent economic thought. Grotius, Pufendorf, the Physiocrats, the Scottish school and the Austrian economists all bear the influence of their writings. Pufendorf recognized the influence of *virtuositas*[69] and utility.[70] He rejected Grotius' Aristotelian analysis that "the most natural measure of the value of each thing is the need of it".[71] If this were the case, he argued, things that serve idle pleasure should

[67] Ibid., p. 144. C.f. with Mariana's quotation on p. 89.

[68] To encourage the immigration of producers, Mariana, for example, recommended the prince to increase taxes on imports. *Biblioteca de Autores Españoles,* Introduction to preliminary discourse, vol. 30, p. xxxv. On this topic see also John Laures, *The Political Economy of Juan de Mariana* (New York: Fordham University, 1928).

[69] "A large diamond, everything else being equal, is more valuable than a small one, although it is not always true in regard to the value of things of a different kind or goodness. Thus, a large dog is not always more valuable than a smaller dog." Pufendorf, *De Jure Naturae,* p. 676.

[70] "The foundation of price in itself is the aptitude of a thing or action, by which it can either mediately or immediately contribute something to the necessity of human life, or to making it more advantageous and pleasant. This is the reason why in ordinary speech things of no use are said to be of no value. . . . So in the fable the cock regarded the pearl, which he had found, of no value, because it was of no use to him [Phaedrus, III. xii]." Ibid.

[71] Hugo Grotius, *De Jure Belli Ac Pacis Libri Ires,* edited by James Brown Scott (New York: Oceana, 1964), bk. II, chap. xii, no. 14.

not have a price, yet "mankind often bestows a price upon such".[72]

The famed Puritan clergyman John Cotton (1584–1652) offers a striking parallel to Late Scholastic thought. John Winthrop reported that in one of Cotton's lectures he listed what he thought should be the rules for trading:

> 1. A man may not sell above the current price, i.e., such a price as is usual in the time and place, and as another (who knows the worth of the commodity) would give for it, if he had occasion to use it; as that is called current money, which every man will take, etc.
>
> 2. When a man loseth in his commodity for want of skill, etc., he must look at it as his own fault or cross, and therefore must not lay it upon another.
>
> 3. Where a man loseth by casualty of sea, or, etc., it is a loss cast upon himself by providence, and he may not ease himself of it by casting it upon another; for so a man should seem to provide against all providences, etc., that he should never lose; but where there is a scarcity of the commodity, there men may raise their price; for now it is a hand of God upon the commodity, and not the person.
>
> 4. A man may not ask any more for his commodity than his selling price, as Ephron to Abraham the land is worth thus much.[73]

These rules could well have been written by any of the Late Scholastics.

The Physiocrats spoke of a "true price" (*le prix veritable*) that could be defined similarly to the Scholastic "just price". They regarded the

---

[72] Pufendorf, *De Jure Naturae,* pp. 676–677. His argument was as follows: "If he [Grotius] means that the foundation of price in itself is want, or that a thing is valued by men merely because they need it, his statement will not hold true universally. For on this theory the price would be taken from things which serve idle pleasure, and yet the boundless luxury of mankind often bestows a price upon such. But we are said actually to need only things without the use of which we must suffer serious inconvenience. See Matthew 5:12. But if he means that the need of the purchaser makes for the raising of price, we confess that such is commonly the case, yet no one of discernment would grant that this is the natural measure of price, so that the more one is straitened by want, the higher the price that can be extorted from him." pp. 676–677.

[73] From John Winthrop's *Journal,* edited by J. K. Hosmer (New York: Scribner's, 1908), vol. 1, pp. 315–318, quoted in Henry William Spiegel, *The Rise of American Economic Thought* (New York: Augustus M. Kelley, 1968), p. 6.

influence of want and need as the foundation of all exchanges and prices. Turgot wrote, "Reciprocal want has led to the exchange of what people have for what they have not."[74] On the other hand, he included other elements in his theory of value and price:

> So long as we consider each exchange as isolated and standing by itself, the value of each of the things exchanged has no other measure than the need or the desire and the means of the contracting parties, balanced one against the other, and it is fixed by nothing but the agreement of their will.[75]

In a book published in 1747, Hutcheson included a short chapter dealing with values or prices and goods. His arguments followed Pufendorf's reasonings.[76] This may be the reason why Adam Smith taught a theory of prices that included many elements of Late-Scholastic thought. Most modern historians declare Adam Smith's theory of value to be based on the production cost of the good.[77] In his *Lectures,* however, Smith's reasoning parallels the Late Scholastics:

> When a buyer comes to the market, he never asks of the seller what expenses he has been at in producing them. The regulation of the market price of goods depends on the following articles:
>
> First, the demand, or need for the commodity. There is no demand for a thing of little *use;* it is not a rational object of *desire.*
>
> Secondly, the abundance or *scarcity* of the commodity in propor-

[74] Turgot, *Reflections,* p. 28.

[75] Ibid., p. 29. According to this Physiocrat, mutual need was the foundation of equivalence in valuation: "I will suppose that one has need of corn, and the other of wine, and that they agree to exchange one bushel of corn for six pints of wine. It is evident that by each of them one bushel of corn is six pints of wine and are looked upon as exactly equivalent, and that in this particular exchange the price of a bushel of corn is six pints of wine, and the price of six pints of wine is a bushel of corn." In the light of the fact that other traders can arrange different prices, however, "Now it is evident that no one of these three prices can be regarded as the true price (*Le prix veritable*)." Ibid., p. 28.

[76] Hutcheson entitled his book *A Short Introduction to Moral Philosophy in Three Books, Containing the Elements of Ethics and the Law of Nature.* Edwin Cannan made this point in his introduction to Adam Smith's *Lectures,* p. xxvi.

[77] Schumpeter espouses this view in his *History of Economic Analysis,* p. 190.

tion to the need of it. If the commodity be scarce, the price is raised, but if the quantity be more than is sufficient to supply the demand, the price falls. Thus it is that diamonds and other precious stones are dear, while iron, which is much more useful, is so many times cheaper, though this depends principally on the last cause, viz.

Thirdly, the riches or poverty of those who demand.[78]

These paragraphs expound a theory of value that is in complete accordance with Late-Scholastic writings. Need, use, desire and scarcity are all terms the Schoolmen used to explain price determination. The third factor Smith mentioned is similar to Conradus' explanation, which the Hispanic Scholastics later adopted. Raymond De Roover noted, "There was nothing basically wrong with the scholastic theory on value and price. It rested on utility and scarcity, and Adam Smith did not improve upon it."[79] This improvement took place only three centuries later with the writings of the Austrian economists. In an article published in 1891, Eugen Böhm-Bawerk described the distinctive qualities of the Austrian economists. He started by stating that "the province of the Austrian economists is *theory* in the strict sense of the word". Regarding the special features that the Austrian school presents in the domain of positive theory, his first point was the theory of value. The theory of marginal (final) utility, as he called it, is the cornerstone of Austrian economic thought. After stating that the idea of value "extends to commodities only when they cannot be had in an abundance which would satisfy all possible demands", F. von Wieser explained the theory of final or *marginal* utility in the following terms:

A commodity is not valued according to the utility which it actually possesses, but by that degree of utility only which is dependant upon that particular commodity, i.e., that degree of utility

[78] Smith, *Lectures,* pp. 176–177. [Italics mine.]

[79] Raymond De Roover, "Scholastic Economics", *Quarterly Journal of Economics* 69 (May 1955): 173; see also Emile Kauder's articles, "The Retarded Acceptance of the Marginal Utility Theory", *Quarterly Journal of Economics* 67 (November 1953): 564–575; and "Genesis of the Marginal Utility School", *Economic Journal* 63 (September 1953): 638–650.

which could not be enjoyed without possessing the commodity in question.[80]

St. Bernardino's example provides a startlingly apt illustration of von Wieser's point. With regard to the comparative price of water and gold in a mountain, it is significant that to forego water could mean foregoing life. St. Bernardino pointed out that water would be more highly esteemed and valued than gold.[81] The Late Scholastics were undoubtedly forerunners of the Austrian school with regard to the theory of economic value.[82] Basing their theory on utility, scarcity and estimation, they offered all the necessary elements to explain the value of economic goods. E. Böhm-Bawerk avowed that one of the most important theoretical problems for an economist to resolve is "the relation between the market price of given goods, and the subjective *estimate* which individuals set upon those goods according to their various wants and inclinations on the one hand and their property and income on the other".[83] According to him, prices (or objective value) are "a resultant of the different subjective estimates of the goods which the buyers and sellers make in accordance with the law of final utility".[84]

The Scholastic Doctors agreed that the government had the right to establish legal prices. They disagreed, however, on the convenience of such price controls. Basing their arguments on utilitarian points of view, most modern economists would not object to the "right" of the

[80] F. von Wieser, "The Theory of Value, A Reply to Professor Macvane", *Annals of the American Academy of Political and Social Science,* II (1891–1892), pp. 600–628, in *Economic Thought: A Historical Anthology,* edited by James A. Gherity (New York: Random House, 1965), p. 315.

[81] See p. 96.

[82] Bernard W. Dempsey pointed out that the Late Scholastics argued against objective theories of economic value "with objections very similar to those which the Austrian school brought against the classical cost analysis". "Just Price in a Functional Economy", *American Economic Review* 25 (September 1935): 483.

[83] E. Böhm-Bawerk, "The Austrian Economists", *Annals of the American Academy of Political and Social Science,* I (1891), pp. 361–384, in *Economic Thought: A Historical Anthology,* p. 288. [Italics mine.]

[84] Ibid., p. 289.

authority to fix prices. Instead, they would argue—like Azpilcueta, Molina or Villalobos—that price fixing is useless, and it would be better to live without it.[85] Although they accept taxes as an inevitable restriction of private property for the sake of protecting it, other libertarians, who employ the natural-law approach, would regard price controls as inadmissible restrictions of property rights.

In cases where the legal price was unjust, the Late Scholastics declared categorically that it did not oblige in conscience. These authors would not undertake *a priori* condemnation of all the dealings that take place today in the "underground economy".[86] Whatever the price fixed by authority, it was assumed to be unjust if it did not cover production costs. The Scholastic moralists were extremely lenient with those who did not obey such laws. They even justified diminishing the weight or the quality of the good in order to compensate for an unjust fixed price.[87]

According to the majority of Classical Liberal authors, an exchange is rendered just by the free will and voluntariness of both parties' participation. The Late Scholastics had a similar stance, but they differed in their definition of a voluntary act. For them, the fact that the transaction took place without overt force was not sufficient proof that both parties had acted with free will. Their discussion centered on Aristotle's dictum that no one willingly suffers an injury (*"volenti non fit injura"*), which is subject to two different interpretations. Addressing the participant in an exchange, the *ex ante* approach scolds, "if you made this transaction of your own free will, then obviously it is because you hoped to gain, so do not complain afterward if you find out that you have made a bad decision."[88] The less-used *ex post* interpretation stipulates that "if, after a transaction,

---

[85] Nonetheless, Ludwig von Mises argues that legal prices are not prices at all. *Human Action,* pp. 392–394.

[86] For a free-market analysis of the underground economy see *The Underground Economy* by Hans F. Sennholz (Auburn, Ala.: Ludwig von Mises Institute of Auburn University, 1984).

[87] Antonio de Escobar y Mendoza, *Universae Theologiae Moralis* (Lyon, 1662), bk. 39, chap. 1, p. 159.

[88] Soto's admonishment of line to the workers is an example. See pp. 126–127.

you find out that you are worse off than before, then the transaction was unjust since no one will voluntarily injure himself". It was implicit in the Scholastic explanation that ignorance on the part of the buyer or the seller could, in certain cases, render the transaction involuntary. Although the Late Scholastics permitted the realization of profit due to better knowledge of the market, they morally condemned those who took advantage of an ignorant consumer.

The Doctors were uncompromising in their condemnation of monopoly.[89] It is important to note that the Schoolmen did not condemn monopolies *per se,* since they did not regard size (being a very large business) or exclusiveness (being the only ones in a specific trade or production branch) as evil qualities. They did censure certain monopolies resulting from official privilege and those monopolies established by secret agreement between merchants or by cornering the market.[90]

Whenever the king allowed a monopoly by granting an exclusive privilege, the Late Scholastic acknowledged the possibility of price abuses. For this reason they recommended that the king fix "fair prices". The only rule that they imagined was cost-plus pricing. It is interesting that cost-plus pricing, which was the norm then, remains so in the case of today's publicly owned monopolies. According to Raymond De Roover, there is no doubt that the conspiracy idea of the antitrust laws goes back to Scholastic precedents and is rooted in the Medieval concept of the just price.[91]

Grotius agreed with Late-Scholastic monopoly theory, specifying that monopolies violate natural law. The only permissible monopolies are (1) those allowed by the king for a just cause and with a fixed

---

[89] De Roover, "Scholastic Economics", p. 184. See also Joseph Höffner, *Wirtschaftsethik und Monopole im Funfzehnten und Sechzehnten Jahrhundert* (Jena, 1941), p. 107.

[90] Joseph Höffner, "Estática y Dinámica en la Etica Económica de la Filosofía Escolástica", *Investigación Económica,* Mexico, 18 (1958): 653.

[91] De Roover, "Monopoly Theory Prior to Adam Smith: A Revision", *Quarterly Journal of Economics* 65 (May 1951): 523–524. There is a substantial difference, however, between the Late Scholastic antimonopoly stance and contemporary antitrust attitudes. The latter focus their attacks on size, positing that largeness can lead to unfairness.

price and (2) those private monopolies that do not charge more than the just price.[92] Of the four types of monopolies the Late Scholastics described,[93] Pufendorf regarded legal monopolies as the only ones that may properly be classified monopolistic:

> A monopoly in the proper sense of the term cannot be established by private citizens, because it has the force of a privilege. For how can a private citizen who has no right to command and cannot use force, directly forbid others, who are also citizens, to deal in a certain kind of merchandise?[94]

Citizens have recourse only to spurious monopolies "maintained by clandestine frauds and conspiracies". Pufendorf listed the activities that could produce such "monopolies": (a) preventing all other citizens from approaching the spot where merchandise is inexpensive, (b) hindering others from bringing their merchandise to the market and (c) cornering the market.[95] He condemned all merchants who employ these means in an attempt to sell at "unjust prices". He also censured those laborers and artisans who agree secretly not to sell their services below a certain price.[96] Although it is based on Late Scholastic thought, Pufendorf's analysis seems to be more in accordance with Classical Liberal conclusions. Twentieth-century libertarians usually condemn only those monopolies established by laws restricting freedom of entry or granting special privileges (such as tax incentives or subsidies). Most modern analysts would agree that direct force and frauds render an exchange involuntary, but cases involving ignorance[97] and monopoly are subject to greater controversy.

---

[92] Grotius, *De Jure Belli Ac Pacis Libri Tres* bk. II, chap. 12, § 16; II, 353; I, 233–234. See also De Roover, "Monopoly Theory", p. 522.

[93] See pp. 116–117.

[94] Pufendorf, *De Jure Naturae,* p. 739.

[95] Ibid., p. 740.

[96] Ibid.

[97] From a strictly positivistic approach, knowledge is a scarce good and, as such, has a market price. Although this is true, no Christian moralist would agree that it is always just to profit from our neighbor's ignorance. Free will *per se* does not make an economic act (or any other human act) morally justifiable. Humans can freely choose to do evil.

Contemporary thought may challenge some of the Late-Scholastics' economic policy recommendations (their acceptance of price controls and their condemnation of monopolies). This is true of both proponents and opponents of the Schoolmen's theoretical principles.

Distributive Justice

Justice was the Scholastics' primary concern.[98] In Aristotelian and Thomist fashion, they perceived that commutative justice dealt with transactions and distributive justice with the distribution of *common* goods. Subsequent critical failure to understand this difference has caused many problems.[99] In our century, theorists often assign such topics as wages, profits and rents, which should be a matter of commutative justice, to the provenance of distributive justice. The development of an economic science based on aggregate analysis may have exacerbated this situation. Such nineteenth-century classical authors as David Ricardo and John Stuart Mill separated the productive process and the factors of production (land, labor and capital) on the one side, placing the distributive process and its forms (rent accruing from land, wages as a reward for labor and profits arising from capital) on the other. Using this framework, moralists began to treat the distributive process as a separate entity in relation to the productive process. Still worse, they dealt with wages, rent and profits as topics of distributive justice, missing the point that in a free society, wages, rents and profits (or losses) stem from the personal exchange of goods and services. Discussion of whether "level" is just should proceed according to the standards of commutative justice.

[98] Although Raymond De Roover wrote that their primary concern was with social justice ("Monopoly Theory", p. 495) the Late Scholastics never used either the term or the concept.

[99] It is difficult to understand how De Roover, in his day the most knowledgeable authority on Medieval economics, could state that distributive justice "regulated the distribution of wealth and income". "Monopoly Theory", p. 495. Neither wages nor profits nor interest (*stipendium, lucrum, usuris*) appears under the heading of distributive justice in any Medieval treatise. They were always considered to be questions of commutative justice.

Just Wages

The Scholastic theory of just wages bears similar flaws and assets to their just price theory. The application of their general theoretical framework to factor-of-production prices was a positive aspect of their analysis. Recognizing that the factors of production are determined by the forces operating in the market, the Doctors dealt with the price of labor (i.e., wages) as equivalent to the price of any other good in the market. They concluded that common estimation in the market plus the interaction of the demand for and supply of labor will produce the just wage.[100]

Pufendorf's train of thought was decidedly similar. In *De Jure Naturae* he declared, "Letting and hiring, whereby the use of an article or labor is furnished another for a price, is similar to buying and selling and is governed by practically the same rules."[101] This approach was also very realistic, for he noted that "whoever is hired when out of work must be content with a modest wage, while he whose services are solicited can value them more highly."[102]

The Late Scholastics were not pessimistic about the effect that the forces of supply and demand might have on wages. Turgot, on the other hand, was one of the first to write that laborers are condemned to subsistence wages. His idea was: "In every kind of work it cannot fail to happen, and as a matter of fact it does happen, that the wages

---

[100] De Roover, *Saint Bernardino and Sant' Antonino,* pp. 23–27.
[101] Pufendorf, *De Jure Naturae,* p. 741.
[102] Ibid., p. 742.

of the workman are limited to what is necessary to procure him his subsistence."[103]

The authors of the Classical school of economics also employed supply-and-demand analysis to describe how wages are determined in the market. Their reasoning, however, did not end with the supply and demand for labor. Working with a labor-theory of value, Ricardo concluded that the "sole cause (apart from the slow fluctuations in the labor market) which fixes the rate of wages is the price of necessaries".[104] Some decades before, Adam Smith had developed a theory of wages containing rudiments of the minimum-of-existence theory.[105] In his *Lectures on Justice,* Smith wrote, "A man then has the natural price of his labour when it is sufficient to maintain him during the time of labour, to defray the expense of education, and to compensate the risk for not living enough, and not succeeding in the business."[106] Smith also endorsed the idea of a wage fund (a portion of capital destined for the maintenance of labor), which John Stuart Mill later developed more extensively.[107]

For the Late Scholastics, wages, profits and rents were a matter of commutative justice. Current economic theory sometimes treats them as a matter of distributive justice.[108] The Classical authors divorced

---

[103] Turgot, *Reflections,* p. 8. According to this Physiocrat, competition among workmen limits wages to subsistence levels. On the other hand, he also recognized that although competition between workers "obliges the man engaged in industry to content himself with a price less than he would like, it is nevertheless certain that this competition has never been numerous enough or keen enough in all different kinds of labours to prevent at any time a man who was more expert, more active, and, above all, more economical than others in his personal consumption, from gaining a little more than was necessary for the subsistence of himself and his family and from saving this surplus to create therewith a little store." Ibid., p. 44.

[104] Thomas De Quincey, "Ricardo Made Easy", *Blackwoods Edinburgh Review* 52 (July–December 1842): 338–353, 457–469, 718–739, in Gherity, *Economic Thought,* p. 195.

[105] Smith, *Wealth of Nations,* p. 71, and Schumpeter, *History of Economic Analysis,* p. 190.

[106] Smith, *Lectures,* p. 176.

[107] Schumpeter, *History of Economic Analysis,* p. 190.

[108] Or as a branch of the more equivocal concept of "social justice". See pp. 120–122, above.

production from distribution theories, specifying that they are governed by different "laws". Their method of analysis—discussing distribution (wages, profits and rents) as respondent to different laws than the ones that affect prices—may have influenced later establishment of differential legal treatment for the prices of commodities and factors of production.[109]

Regarding the advisability of a different wage for different types of jobs, Adam Smith's reasonings were similar to those of St. Bernardino:

> The wages of labour vary with the ease or hardship, the cleanliness or dirtiness, the honourableness or dishonourableness of the employment. Thus in most places, take the year round, a journey man tailor earns less than a journey man weaver. His work is much easier.[110]

Smith also pointed out the influence that educational requisites exert on wages:

> In the different trades there must be a considerable difference, because some trades, such as those of the tailor and weaver, are not learned by casual observation and a little experience, like that of the day-labourer, but take a great deal of time and pains before they are acquired.[111]

Declaring that wages should be high enough to repay the laborer for the expense of his ten or twelve years of education, he specified that watchmakers, for example, should earn more than day laborers.[112] Smith also quoted Mandeville as another author who ascribed greater importance to scarcity than to usefulness for the determination of prices and wages.[113]

[109] On the influence of economic theory on economic policy see pp. 35–39, above.

[110] Smith, *Lectures,* p. 100.

[111] Ibid., p. 174.

[112] Ibid. Adam Smith cited R. Cantillon's *Essai sur la nature du commerce en general* (1755), pp. 23–24. He included the same thoughts in *Wealth of Nations,* pp. 106–107.

[113] "Scarcity enhances the price of things much oftener than the usefulness of them. Hence it is evident why those arts and sciences will always be the most lucrative that cannot be attained to but in great length of time, by tedious study and close application." Mandeville, *Fable of the Bees,* pt. ii. Dialogue vi, p. 423, quoted in Smith, *Lectures,* p. 175.

Adam Smith's analysis stems from his cost-of-production theory of value. After writing that *"caeteris paribus,* the jobs that require more labor, danger, art and industry are more highly esteemed by the community", St. Bernardino arrived at a similar conclusion.[114] Nonetheless, it is not inconsistent with a theory of value based on subjective utility to speak about the importance of cost in price determination.[115]

The Scholastic Doctors did not limit their discussion of wage determination to the issues of supply, demand and cost. Sylvestre stated that the prices of productive goods (*rei fructuosa*) should depend on the revenue (*reditus*) that could be expected from them. This may be regarded as an implicit imputation theory, the same one that the Austrian school employed to explain the value of the means of production. Friedrich von Wieser is credited as being the first to use the term *imputation* to describe the concept that "the degree of utility possessed by the means of production depends entirely upon the degree of utility of the commodities produced by means of them and is based upon this."[116] Wieser added that, according to the view of the Austrian school,

> the estimation of value should begin like the estimation of utility, upon which it is based, with the products, and proceed thence to the means of production. The consequence of this is that the utility and value of the means of production prove to be no more identical than the utility and value of the products.[117]

Wieser applied this theory both to labor and to its price. He stated that the scarcity of labor and its productivity help to determine wages. Labor can therefore command a price even when it involves "no expenditure of effort whatever".[118] According to Wieser, human esteem is an essential element in the theory of value and price (including

---

[114] St. Bernardino of Siena *Opera Omnia* (Venice, 1591), chap. III, art. 2, p. 338.

[115] According to F. von Wieser, cost is "nothing but a complicated form of value in use". "Theory of Value", p. 319.

[116] Ibid., p. 316.

[117] Ibid. [Italics mine.]

[118] Ibid.

the price of labor). A productive good "loses its value so soon as this [the good it produces] ceases to be esteemed".[119]

Wieser judged that "it is a fact of highest importance that the value of productive property and of productive powers anticipates the expected value of the commodities". This dictum is very similar to Sylvestre's declaration that the price of a fruitful good must depend on the revenue that can be derived from it. In Wieser's words, we must take into account the "full value of the fruits expected".[120]

Wieser's theory does not allow the conclusion that if the goods produced cannot be sold, then the laborer should not be paid. According to Late-Scholastic doctrine, as well, all agreed-upon wages must be paid in fulfillment of the contract. In this case, it is the tradesmen and businessmen who must bear the loss.[121] For the same reason, in a case where the goods can be sold at a price that far exceeds costs, the businessman may keep all the profits and need not share them with the owners of the other factors of production (including labor).

The Late Scholastics would regard a situation in which the laborers share in the profits as a sort of partnership. They favored this type of profit sharing only if the same procedure applied to losses. As did the Late Scholastics, Adam Smith condemned unfair practices in the labor market, avowing that the law should punish conspiracies on the part of the masters with the same severity with which it castigates workers' agreements.[122] Although both Smith and St. Antonino acknowledged payment of wages in money or in kind, the Scottish economist stated that "the law which obliges the masters in several different trades to pay their workmen in money and not in goods, is quite just and equitable."[123] In addition, he rejected

[119] Ibid.

[120] Ibid., pp. 321–322.

[121] See p. 133.

[122] "When masters combine together in order to reduce the wages of their workmen, they commonly enter into a private bond or agreement, not to give more than a certain wages under a certain penalty. Were the workmen to enter into a contrary combination of the same kind, not to accept of a certain wage under a certain penalty, the law would punish them very severely; and if it dealt impartially, it would treat the masters in the same manner." Smith, *Wealth of Nations*, p. 142.

[123] Ibid.

truck payments made without the request or consent of the work-men.[124]

In matters of economic policy, Austrian economists consistently opposed the use of force in society for other than defensive reasons. They therefore rejected any attempt, either by workers or employers, to use force to impose a wage differing from the one established by the market. Almost every free-market economist has condemned coercive labor-union actions. There are, however, mixed feelings regarding labor-union activity *per se*. The Classical authors were sometimes more contemptuous toward employers than toward labor combinations.[125]

The concept of family wage has become very important in contemporary economic policy. The Schoolmen explicitly denounced the proposal that the just wage should be determined according to the needs of the laborers or the needs of their families.[126] They did not ignore the issue of a family wage; they simply rejected it on the grounds that it contradicts their theory that the just wage is set by common estimation in the absence of fraud.[127] Classical Liberal economists would also agree with the dictum that the laborer

[124] Ibid. Of the Late Scholastics, St. Antonino dealt most extensively with unfair practices in the labor market. He fervently opposed the payment of wages in kind when the contract called for payment in cash. *Summa de Conffession* (n.p.), p. CXVII and p. CXVIII. (This old, diminutive Spanish edition of excerpts of Antonino's writings is the property of the library of the Cathedral of Toledo in Spain. These same remarks appear in Antonino's *Summa Theologica*, pt. II, titulo I, chap. 17, § 8.)

[125] See Hans F. Sennholz, "Ideological Roots of Unionism", *The Freeman* 34, (February 1984): 107–120.

[126] See p. 126.

[127] See Wilhelm Weber, *Wirtshaftsethik am Vorabend des Liberalismus* (Aschendorff, Munster Westf., 1959). In *St. Bernardino of Siena and Sant' Antonino*, p. 26, Raymond De Roover argued that "the system of family allowances was born in the twentieth century. To project it into the Middle Ages is simply an anachronism or wishful thinking."

has nothing to complain about if he was paid according to a contract to which both employer and employee gave their free consent.[128]

Profits

The Medieval Schoolmen dealt with business profits and the reward for labor in separate chapters of their works. Nonetheless, they sometimes regarded as business profits what contemporary economists would consider the reward for labor.[129] Modern economists define pure business or entrepreneurial profits as those that the entrepreneur earns due to his correct anticipation of future market conditions. In this sense, profits can only be construed as a reward for entrepreneurial labor if the latter is defined as the job of anticipating the consumers' desires and the market conditions with certitude. It is significant that accurate predictions concerning the future are implicit in the Late-Scholastic justification of profits that accrue from purchase and sale at just prices (i.e., market prices). They cited the example of a merchant who bought a good in a region where it was inexpensive and abundant in order to sell it in another region where he expected the price to be high. Depending on the correctness of his expectations, he would either reap profits or suffer loss. The Late Scholastics believed

---

[128] For those who ascribe to the misleading legend that the Scholastics were apologists for the status quo, it is convenient to remember the types of labor laws enacted in Medieval Europe. In Great Britain in 1563, Queen Elizabeth passed the famous "Statute of Artificers" legitimizing *forced* labor. This statute provided that: "(1) whoever had worked on the land until the age of 12 be compelled to remain there and not leave for work at any other trade; (2) all craftsmen, servants, and apprentices who had no great reputation in their fields be forced to harvest wheat; and (3) unemployed persons were compelled to work as agricultural laborers. In addition, the statute prohibited any worker from quitting his job unless he had a license proving that he had already been hired by another employer. And, furthermore, justices of the peace were ordered to set maximum wage rates, geared to changes in the cost of living." Quoted by Murray Rothbard in *Essays on Liberty,* XI (Irvington-on-Hudson, N.Y.: Foundation for Economic Education, 1964), p. 182.

[129] Hans Sennholz would consider it a remuneration for managerial labor. *Death and Taxes,* p. 14.

that, regardless of his costs and labor, the merchant ought to keep the profits arising from such a trade. They explicitly rejected the idea that costs, risk and labor justify profits. Since profits are justifiable so long as they are obtained by buying and selling at market prices, the Schoolmen rejected the viability of a legal limit on profits. It was for this same reason that they descried the fixing of profits in accordance with production costs. In the belief that business (both production and trading) should be open to profit and loss, the Doctors declared the whole idea of earning profits without incurring risks to be completely unnatural, and they censured the businessman who calls on the government for help.

Classical Liberal authors have also condemned such an attitude. Ludwig von Mises realized that an entrepreneur's efforts to secure profits may lead him to excess:

> If he is concerned for the fate of his successors and wants to consolidate his property for them in a way contrary to the interests of the community, he will have to become an enemy of the capitalist social order and demand every kind of restriction on competition. . . . Consideration for his own property and for the property of his successors may, therefore, urge the entrepreneurs rather to support than to oppose Socialism. . . . [Entrepreneurs] have an interest in combining to carry through tariff and other restrictions which conflict with the essence and principle of Liberalism or to resist government interference which may injure them.[130]

Declaring that profits are allowable even when the object of the transaction could be deemed immoral, the Doctors legitimization of gambling leaves the door open for justification of any kind of entrepreneurial profits. The same can be said with reference to the Schoolmen's attitude toward a prostitute's earnings.[131]

---

[130] Mises, *Socialism,* p. 455.

[131] Modern economists would regard the earnings of a prostitute as remuneration for her specific kind of labor and not as profits. The Late Scholastics, however, used the term *profits* (*lucrum*) to describe such income. (See, for example, p. 138.)

Interest and Banking

Late-Scholastic interest doctrine cannot be regarded as a decisive factor in the development of later theories that justify interest payments. Nonetheless, with their emphasis on the fact that "present money has more value than absent money" and their tenet that money can be regarded as a productive good, some late Medieval authors might have suggested a positive attitude toward interest payments,[132] had they not stipulated that such arguments were not sufficient to counterbalance their criticism of commercial activities, including interest payments. Father Felipe de La Cruz is the exception to this rule. Although La Cruz was very careful and scholarly in citing other Late Scholastics, he cannot be regarded as a typical exponent of Late-Scholastic interest theory.[133]

Pufendorf's ideas concerning interest rates are similar to those La Cruz espoused. Avowing that, by the aid of men's industry, money is "made most productive in securing for itself things that are fruitful both in nature and for the state",[134] he declared, "Nor is it contrary to nature to rent one's own property to others."[135]

As a seminary graduate, Turgot was greatly influenced by theological doctrines.[136] He disagreed with those who opposed interest payments, devoting an entire chapter of his *Reflections* to the refutation of the Schoolmen's errors in this regard.[137] Stating first that "it is for want of having looked at lending on interest in its true light that certain moralists, more rigid than enlightened, have endeavoured

---

[132] According to T. F. Divine, "Abbe Ferdinando Galiani in 1750 stated correctly the importance of the time preference as a determinant of the rate of interest. This concept, repeated by Anne Robert Turgot, was fully developed in the 1880s by Böhm-Bawerk." *New Catholic Encyclopedia,* vol. VII, s.v. "Interest".

[133] See p. 141.

[134] Pufendorf, *De Jure Naturae,* p. 757.

[135] Ibid., p. 758.

[136] Turgot was a Roman Catholic. In 1747 he received a Bachelor of Theology degree from the Seminaire de Saint-Suplice.

[137] Turgot, *Reflections,* § LXXIII, "Errors of the Schoolmen refuted". pp. 68–70.

to make us regard it [the interest] as a crime",[138] Turgot repeated
the argument that money could be "productive":

> Money considered as a physical substance, as a mass of metal, does
> not produce anything; but money employed in advances for enter-
> prises . . . procures a definite profit.[139]

Turgot's justification of interest payments, however, rested on the
belief that the owner of money can do what he pleases with it. He
declared that if the borrower agrees to pay the interest the lender
demands, then it is clear that both believe that the exchange will be
profitable.[140]

The teachings of the English classical economists John Locke, Adam
Smith, David Ricardo and John Stuart Mill lent greater support to the
attribution of legitimacy to interest rates. They all regarded the
payment of interest as a natural phenomenon. The Austrian economists,
on the other hand, achieved a better understanding of the essence of
interest payments. They reasoned that natural interest rates — or
"originary interest", in Böhm-Bawerk's words — arise from the fact
that human beings place a higher value on a good in the present than
on the same good in the future. This time-preference theory regards
interest as something inherent to human nature.[141] Many years after its
first edition, the main work in this field is still *Capital and Interest* by
Eugene Böhm-Bawerk. Other Austrian economists, especially Ludwig
von Mises, later improved and expanded Böhm-Bawerk's theories.

In his criticism of earlier interest theory, Böhm-Bawerk devoted a
chapter to Medieval and Late Medieval doctrines. Not only did he
quote and criticize St. Thomas Aquinas' ideas, but also the support
that some Late Scholastics authors lent to Thomist theories. Specifically,
Böhm-Bawerk attacked Covarrubias y Leiva. It is worthy of note that
Böhm-Bawerk's relegated his mention of the Schoolmen's recognition

---

[138] Ibid., p. 68.

[139] Ibid., p. 69.

[140] Ibid., p. 71.

[141] "Interest ultimately flows from human nature. Men of all ages and races value
their present cash more highly than a claim payable in the future." Sennholz, *Death
and Taxes,* p. 14.

that "present money has a higher value than absent money" to a footnote.[142] The works of those theorists who advanced the understanding of interest rates do not indicate that the Late Scholastics aided their reasoning. It is easier to see them as the early proponents of a long-espoused condemnation of interest payments.[143] This is not to say that Late-Medieval economic thought is to blame for the backwardness of interest theory. No one group of scholars can be expected to produce solutions for all the intellectual problems they encounter. The Late Scholastics' inability to formulate a consistent and coherent theory of interest does not negate their other contributions, else we should be forced to disregard Classical economic teachings due to the errors inherent in their theory of the value of economic goods.

Although lack of resolution of the interest rate problem led to insufficient analysis of banking functions, some Scholastic reasonings in this regard are of considerable interest to the modern economist. Molina's statement that bankers' only legal obligation is to have the money ready when their clients request it could contribute to arguments promoting "free banking" and attacking coercive reserve requirements. Still, it is difficult to speak of banking freedom when interest payments are forbidden by law.

De Roover argued that since lending with interest was proscribed, "the bankers found another way of making profits—by dealing in foreign exchange". He recognized that "because of the slowness of communications", the purchase of a foreign draft "always involved granting credit as well as dealing in exchange".[144] Indeed, banks can bury

---

[142] Böhm-Bawerk, *Capital and Interest,* p. 14.

[143] Mises, *Socialism,* p. 377.

[144] *International Encyclopedia of the Social Sciences,* s.v. "Economic Thought", by Raymond De Roover. The same author wrote that "such a contract involved an advance of funds in one place and its repayment in another place, and, usually in other currency. Technically it was not a loan, so the bankers were able to lend money at a profit without being branded as usurers. The usury doctrine, therefore, did not prevent the development of banking but changed its course because exchange dealings were licit and discounting was not." *New Catholic Encyclopedia,* s.v. "Scholastic Economics".

interest payments in their foreign-exchange dealings, but it must be noted that such "under-the-table" operations betray a negative attitude toward the act of borrowing money for a price. For this reason, it is much safer to conclude with De Roover that "the great weakness of scholastic economics was the usury doctrine,"[145] and to disagree with J. A. Schumpeter's comment that these authors "launched the theory of interest".[146]

---

[145] De Roover, "Scholastic Economics", p. 173.
[146] Schumpeter, *History of Economic Analysis,* p. 101.

13

CONCLUSION

It cannot be proven that all Late-Scholastic writings favored the free market. Nor may we conclude that one must be a Classical Liberal to be a good Christian. The fact that saintly people espouse a certain opinion does not guarantee its certitude. The above analysis of the Schoolmen's writings suggests that modern free-market authors owe the Scholastics more than they imagine. The same can be said for Western civilization.

In this light, this study omits several interesting historical questions. For example, if the Roman Catholic Late-Scholastics were so much in favor of a free society, why then did capitalism evolve more rapidly and pervasively in countries with a Protestant majority? After the French Revolution, large numbers of intellectuals rejected faith. At the same time, many of the faithful rejected reason. Might the rivalry between the Church and the "liberals" have arisen from these diametrically opposed positions?

For the majority of Classical Liberals, the most important point in economic science is the subjective theory of value. Declaring that essential laws are those that protect private property, they established freedom as standard for all ethical judgments.

Late-Scholastic recommendations lead to similar conclusions. They differ only in reference to the rules governing ethical judgments. The Schoolmen believed freedom to be an essential element in Christian ethics. They specified, however, that the goodness or badness of human actions must be judged in relation to the goal of human existence: God. In Christian ethics, good actions are those that drive men nearer to God. Evil actions are those that pull men away from their Creator.

If Late-Scholastic analyses are true, our civilization is in danger. Private property is under attack even by many who claim to be its defenders. A society guaranteeing peace and freedom cannot survive without the institution of private property.

Current events are not a result of a mysterious design—they are the result of human action. Economists, moralists and politicians share responsibility for the actual trend of developments. Their ideas are influencing and "making" history. Western civilization is bound to lose its freedom if the moralists and economists do not recognize and understand the benefits of a free society. The enemies of the property order carry the banners of human rights, justice and morality. Paradoxically, these mottos conflict with their idea of society. Suppression and severe limitation of the use of private property are turning productive lands into wastelands, social cooperation into class conflict and, what is worse, free people into slaves.

Yet creeping darkness increases the awareness of light. In many regions of the world, freedom lovers are repossessing the banners of morality from undeserving hands. People are attaching increasing importance to the ethical rather than the material benefits of a private-property order. In this context, Late-Scholastic writings are an old source that can still produce fresh thoughts.

Private property is rooted in human freedom, which is founded in human nature, which, like any other nature, is created by God. Private property is the essential prerequisite for economic freedom. Many people are currently attempting to dry up its roots. It will take a new wave of Scholastic thought to save them, to return the plant of civilization to its natural fruitfulness.

SELECTED BIBLIOGRAPHY

Books

Albornóz, Bartolomé de. *Arte de los Contratos.* Valencia, 1573.

Alcalá, Luis de. *Tractado de los préstamos que passan entre mercaderes y tractantes, y por consiguiente de los logros, cambios, compras adelantadas, y ventas al fiado.* Toledo: Juan de Ayala, 1543.

Antoine, Gabriel. *Theologia Moralis Universa.* Cracovia, 1774.

Antonino of Florence, St. *Repertorium totius summe auree domini Antonini Archipresulis florentini ordinis predicatoris [Summa Theologica].* Lyon, Johannis Cleyn, 1516.

Aquinas, St. Thomas. *Summa Theologica.* London: Blackfriars, 1975.

Aragón, Pedro de. *De Iustitia et Iure.* Lyon, 1596.

Augustine, St. *City of God.* London: Penguin, 1972.

Azpilcueta, Martín de. *Manual de Confesores y Penitentes.* Coimbra, 1553, and Salamanca, 1556.

Baldwin, John W. *Medieval Theories of the Just Price: Romanists, Canoninsts, and Theologians in the 12th and 13th Centuries.* Philadelphia: American Philosophical Society, 1959.

Bañez, Domingo de. *De Iustitia et Iure Decisiones.* Salamanca, 1594.

Bernardino of Siena, St. *Opera Omnia.* Venice, 1591.

Böhm-Bawerk, Eugen. *Capital and Interest.* South Holland, Ill.: Libertarian Press, 1959.

Chafuen, Alejandro A. et al. *Cristianismo y Libertad.* Buenos Aires: Fundación para el Avance de la Educación, 1984.

Covarrubias y Leiva, Diego. *Opera Omnia.* Salamanca, 1577.

Cravero, Jose Mario Juan. *La Ley Natural en la Filosofía Económica de Fray Tomás de Mercado (d. 1575).* Biblioteca del Pensamiento

Económico Latinoamericano del Periodo Hispano (Bibleh), Consejo Nacional de Investigaciones Científicas y Técnicas (Conicet), Serie Ensayos y Conferencias, No. 2. Buenos Aires: Facultad de Ciencias Sociales y Económicas de la Pontificia Universidad Católica Argentina Santa María de los Buenos Aires, 1983.

Dempsey, Bernard W. *Interest and Usury.* Washington, D.C.: American Council on Public Affairs, 1943.

Escobar y Mendoza, Antonio de. *Universae Theologiae Moralis.* Lyon, 1662.

Fanfani, Amintore. *Le Origini dello Spirito Capitalistico in Italia.* Milan: Vita e Pensiero, 1933.

Finnis, John. *Natural Law and Natural Rights.* Oxford: Clarendon Press, 1980.

García, Francisco. *Tratado Utilísimo de Todos los Contratos, Quantos en los Negocios Humanos se Pueden Ofrecer.* Valencia, 1583.

Grice-Hutchinson, Marjorie. *Early Economic Thought in Spain, 1177–1740.* London: Allen & Unwin, 1975.

——. *The School of Salamanca: Readings in Spanish Monetary History, 1544–1605.* Oxford: Clarendon Press, 1952.

Grotius, Hugo. *De Jure Belli Ac Pacis Libri Tres.* Edited by James Brown Scott. New York: Oceana, 1964.

Hamilton, Bernice. *Political Thought in Sixteenth-Century Spain.* Oxford: Clarendon Press, 1963.

Höffner, Joseph. *Statik und Dynamik in der Scholastischen Wirtschaftsethik.* Cologne: Westdeutscherverlag, 1955.

——. *Wirtschaftsethik und Monopole im funfzehnten und sechzehnten Jahrhundert.* Jena: Gustav Fischer, 1941.

Iparraguirre, Demetrio. *Francisco de Vitoria, una Teoría Social del Valor Económico.* Publicaciones de la Universidad de Deusto, 1st series, vol. 8. Bilbao: Mensajero del Corazon de Jesus, 1957.

La Cruz, Felipe de. *Tratado Unico de Intereses Sobre si se Puede Llevar Dinero por Prestallo.* Madrid: Francisco Martinez, 1637.

Laures, John. *The Political Economy of Juan de Mariana.* New York: Fordham University Press, 1928.

Ledesma, Pedro de. *Summa.* Salamanca, 1614.

Lessio, Leonardo. *De Iustitia et Iure.* Antwerp, 1626.

Lugo, Juan de. *De Iustitia et Iure.* Lyon, 1642.

Mariana, Juan de. *Del Rey y de la Institución Real.* In *Biblioteca de Autores Españoles,* Rivadeneyra, vol. 31. Madrid: Editions Atlas, 1950.

———. *Tratado sobre la Moneda de Vellón.* In *Biblioteca de Autores Españoles,* Rivadeneyra, vol. 31. Madrid: Editions Atlas, 1950.

Medina, Juan de. *De Contractibus.* Salamanca, 1550.

Menger, Carl. *Problems of Economics and Sociology.* Urbana, University of Illinois Press, 1963.

Mercado, Tomás de. *Summa de Tratos y Contratos.* Seville, 1571, and 1594, New ed. Madrid: Editora Nacional, 1975.

Mises, Ludwig von. *Human Action: A Treatise on Economics.* New Haven, Conn.: Yale University Press, 1949.

———. *Socialism.* Indianapolis: Liberty Press, 1981.

———. *Theory and History.* New Haven, Conn.: Yale University Press, 1957.

Molina, Luis de. *De Iustitia et Iure.* Moguntiae, 1614, and Madrid: Ed. Nacíonal, 1981.

Navarra, Pedro de. *De Restitutione.* Toledo, 1597.

Navarrete, Pedro Fernandez. *Conservación de Monarquias.* Madrid, 1619.

Popper, Karl. *The Open Society and Its Enemies.* Princeton: Princeton University Press, 1950.

Robertson, H. M. *Aspects of the Rise of Economic Individualism: A Criticism of Max Weber and His School.* New ed. Clifton: A. M. Kelly, 1973.

Saavedra Fajardo, Diego de. *Idea de un Príncipe Pólitico-Cristiano.* In *Biblioteca de Autores Españoles,* Rivadeneyra, vol. 25. Madrid: Editions Atlas, 1947.

Salón, Miguel. *Commentariorum in Disputationem de Iustitia Quam Habet D. Tho. Secunda Sectione Secundae partis suae Summa Theologicae.* Valencia, 1591.

Saravia de la Calle, Luis. *Instrucción de Mercaderes.* Introduction by Pablo Ruiz de Alda. Madrid, 1949.

Schumpeter, Joseph A. *Economic Doctrine and Method.* New York: Oxford University Press, 1954.

———. *History of Economic Analysis.* New York: Oxford University Press, 1954.

Sennholz, Hans F. *Age of Inflation.* Belmont, Mass.: Western Islands, 1979.

———. *Death and Taxes.* Washington, D.C.: Heritage Foundation, 1976.

Sennholz, Mary. *Faith and Freedom: A Biographical Sketch of a Great American, John Howard Pew.* Grove City, Penn.: Grove City College, 1975.

Sierra Bravo, Restituto. *El Pensamiento Social y Económico de la Escolástica: Desde sus Orígenes al Comienzo del Catolicismo Social.* 2 vol. Madrid: Consejo Superior de Investigaciones Científicas, 1975.

Smith, Adam. *An Inquiry into the Nature and Causes of the Wealth of Nations.* 1776. New York: Modern Library, 1937.

———. *Lectures on Justice, Police, Revenue and Arms, Delivered in the University of Glasgow by Adam Smith, Reported by a Student in 1763.* New York: Kelley & Millman, 1956.

Soto, Domingo de. *De Iustitia et Iure.* Madrid: IEP, 1968.

———. *Deliberación acerca la Causa de los Pobres.* New ed. Madrid: Instituto de Estudios Políticos, 1965.

———. *Deliberación en la Causa de los Pobres.* Salamanca, 1545.

Turgot, Anne Robert Jacques. *Reflections on the Formation and the Distribution of Riches.* New York: Macmillan, 1914.

Villalobos, Henrique de. *Summa de la Theologia Moral y Canónica.* Barcelona, 1632.

Villalón, Cristobal de. *Provechoso Tratado de Cambios y Contrataciones de Mercaderes y Reprobación de Usura.* Valladolid: Francisco Fernandez de Cordoba, 1542.

Vitoria, Francisco de. *De Indis et de Iure Belli Relectiones.* Edited by Ernest Nys. New York: Oceana, 1964.

——. *De Justitia.* 3 vol. Edited by Beltrán de Heredia. Madrid: Publicaciones de la Asociación Francisco de Vitoria, 1934–1936.

Weber, Wilhelm. *Wirtshaftsethik am Vorabend des Liberalismus.* Aschendorff, Munster Westf, 1959.

Articles

Chafuen, Alejandro A., "Argumentos post-tomistas en favor de la propiedad privada". *Libertas* 3 (October 1985): 179–197.

——. "Justicia distributiva en la escolastica tardia". *Estudios Publicos* 18 (1985): 5–20.

——. "Las ideas economicas de Fray Pedro Aguado (c. 1538–c. 1589)". Buenos Aires, Programa Bibleh-CONICET, UCA (1978): 27–82.

——. "Contribuciones de los frailes de la Orden de Santo Domingo en la Isla La Española (1510–1519)". Buenos Aires, Programa Bibleh-CONICET, UCA (1980): 1–22.

——. "Moral y economia". In *Liberalismo y Sociedad.* Buenos Aires: Macchi (1984), pp. 82–99.

Dempsey, Bernard W. "Just Price in a Functional Economy". *American Economic Review* 25 (September 1935): 471–486.

De Roover, Raymond. "The Concept of the Just Price: Theory and Economic Policy". *Journal of Economic History* 18 (December 1958): 418–434.

——. "Scholastic Economics: Survival and Lasting Influence from the Sixteenth Century to Adam Smith". *Quarterly Journal of Economics* 69 (May 1955): 161–190.

International Encyclopedia of the Social Sciences. New York: Free Press,

1968. S.v. "Economic Thought, Ancient and Medieval Thought", by Raymond De Roover.

Kauder, Emil. "Genesis of the Marginal Utility School". *The Economic Journal* 63 (September 1953): 638–650.

———. "The Retarded Acceptance of the Marginal Utility Theory". *The Quarterly Journal of Economics* 67 (November 1953): 564–575.

New Catholic Encyclopedia, New York: McGraw-Hill, 1967. S.v. "Scholasticism", by I. C. Brady.

———. *S.v. "Scholastic Method", by J. A. Weisheipl.*

Popescu, Oreste. "Aspectos Analíticos en la Doctrina del Justo Precio de Juan de Matienzo (1520–1579)". In *La Economia Como Disciplina Cientifica. Ensayos en Honor del Profesor Dr. Francisco Valsechi* (Buenos Aires: Macchi, 1982), pp. 235–286.

Sennholz, Hans F. "Ideological Roots of Unionism". *The Freeman* 34 (February 1982): 107–120.

Veatch, Henry B. "Natural Law: Dead or Alive". *Literature of Liberty* 1 (October–December 1978): 7–31.

INDEX OF PROPER NAMES

INDEX OF SUBJECTS